John Fletcher

Bibliography of Minnesota

John Fletcher

Bibliography of Minnesota

ISBN/EAN: 9783337717322

Printed in Europe, USA, Canada, Australia, Japan

Cover: Foto ©ninafisch / pixelio.de

More available books at **www.hansebooks.com**

BIBLIOGRAPHY OF MINNESOTA.

PREPARED BY THE LIBRARIAN OF THE SOCIETY.

NOTE.

While I have ventured to call this article a "Bibliography of Minnesota," its peculiar arrangement, departing as it does, somewhat from the usual rules of Bibliography, may weaken its claim to that title. It is little more, in reality, than a transcript of the Catalogue of that portion of the Library of the Minnesota Historical Society, which relates to this State. The collection of works and publications on that subject now in possession of the Society, is so nearly complete, that it contains almost every work which can be said to strictly belong to a Bibliography of Minnesota, in addition to a large number—(not, however, included in this paper)—which have such intimate relations to the subject, they might reasonably have been embraced in it, had not the list threatened to consume too much space.

I have arranged the titles by subjects, believing that this plan will best show at a glance what has been printed in any one class or division; while numerous cross-references, and an index of authors, will, I trust, remedy any defects which that plan may have. It will be remarked, also, that all works are arranged chronologically.

This is the first attempt to collect and publish a list of works relating to Minnesota. It will be a matter of surprise to many, even of our own citizens, that so much has been printed—here and elsewhere—relating to a State organized as a separate commonwealth only twenty-one years ago; and it is sent forth in the hope that it may prove some aid to Librarians and Bibliographers in other States, no less than to our own citizens.   J. F. W.

EARLY EXPLORATIONS AND TRAVELS,

Made prior to the organization of Minnesota as a Territory in 1849.

VOYAGE OU NOUVELLE DECOUVERTE d' un Tres Grand Pays dans L' Amerique, entre le nouveau Mexique et la mer glaciale,

par le R. P. Louis Hennepin; Avec toutes les particularitez
de ce Pais, & de celui connu sous le nom de LA LOUISIANE;
les avantages qui on en peut tirer par l' establissement des
Colonies enrichie de Cartes Geographiques. Augmente de
quelques figures en taille douce. Avec un voyage qui contient
une Relation exacte de l' Origine, Mœurs, Coustumes, Religion,
Guerres & Voyages des Caraibes, Sauvages des Isles Antilles
de L' AMERIQUE, Faite par le Sieur De La Borde, Tiree du
Cabinet de Monsr. Blondel, Amsterdam. Chez Adriaan
Braakman, Marchand Libraire pres le Dam, 1704, 16°: pp.
xxxiv, 604, [2 maps, 6 engravings.]

MEMOIRE SUR LES MŒURS, Coustumes et Relligion des Sauvages de L' Amerique Septentrionale, par Nicolas Perrot; Publie
pour la Premiere fois par le R. P. J. Tailhan, de la Compagnie
de Jesus. Leipzig & Paris, Librairie A. Franck. Albert L.
Herold, 1864, 12°: pp. VIII, 341, XLIII.
[See Collections of Minn. Histor. Soc., Pg. 22.]

NEW VOYAGES TO NORTH AMERICA, giving a full account of the
Customs, Commerce, Religion, and Strange Opinions of the
Savages of that Country, with POLITICAL REMARKS upon the
Courts of *Portugal* and *Denmark*, and the present State of the
Commerce of those Countries. The Second Edition, Written
by the Baron LAHONTAN, Lord-Lieutenant of the *French* Colony
at *Placentia* in *Newfoundland;* Now in *England.* LONDON:
Printed for J. Walthoe, J. and J. Bonwicke, J. Osborn, S. Birt,
T. Ward, and E. Wicksteed, 1735. Two vols., 12°. Vol. I,
pp. xxiv, 280. [2 maps; 4 plates.] Vol. II, pp. 302. [3
maps; 9 plates.]

THE DISCOVERY OF THE GREAT WEST; by Francis Parkman.
Boston: Little, Brown & Co., 1869, 8°: pp. 425.
[This work covers the period from 1643 to 1689.]

HISTORICAL COLLECTIONS OF LOUISIANA AND FLORIDA, inclu-
ding Translations of original manuscripts relating to their
Discovery and Settlement, with numerous Historical and
Biographical Notes. By B. F. French. New Series. New
York: J. Sabin & Sons, 84 Nassau street, 1869, 8°: pp. 362.

THE HISTORY OF LOUISIANA, or of the Western Parts of
Virginia and Carolina: Containing a Description of the

Countries that lye on both Sides of the River Mississippi : With an Account of the Settlements, Inhabitants, Soil, Climate and Products. Translated from the French, (lately published) by M. Le Page Du Pratz ; with some Notes and Observations relating to our Colonies. In Two Volumes. London : MDCC,- LXIII, 16°. Vol. I, pp. VI, 368 ; [map.] Vol. II : pp. VI, 272 [map.]

HISTORICAL COLLECTIONS OF LOUISIANA, embracing Translations of many rare and valuable Documents relating to the Natural, Civil and Political History of that State, etc. Part IV. Redfield, New York : 1852. 8° pp. 268. [Map.]

[Entitled "Discovery and Explorations of the Mississippi ;" contains Original Narratives of Marquette, Allouez, Membre, Hennepin and Douay.]

EARLY VOYAGES UP AND DOWN THE MISSISSIPPI. By Cavalier, St. Cosme, LeSueur, Gravier and Guignas. With an introduction and Notes. [By John G. Shea.] Albany : 1861, 4° : pp. 191.

HISTOIRE ET DESCRIPTION GENERALE DE LA NOUVELLE FRANCE, avec le Journal Historique d' un Voyage fait par ordre du Roi dans L' Amerique Septentrionnale. Par le P. De Charlevoix de la Compagnie de Jesus, a Paris, M. DCC. XLIV. Avec Approbation et Privilege du Roi. Three Volumes, 4° : pp. XXVI, 664 ; XVI, 582 and 56 ; XIV, 543.

TRAVELS THROUGH THE INTERIOR PARTS OF NORTH AMERICA in the years 1766, 1767 and 1768. By J. Carver, Esq., Captain of a Company of Provincial Troops during the late War with France. Illustrated with copper plates, coloured. The third edition. To which is added, some account of the Author and a Copious Index. London : MDCCLXXXI. 8° pp. 564. [2 maps, 5 engravings.]

—— Do. Another edition, published by Isaiah Thomas & Co., Walpole, N. H., 1813 ; 16° : pp. 280.

—— Do. Another edition, entitled " Carver's Travels in Wisconsin." New York : Printed by Harper & Brothers, No. 82, Cliff Street, 1838 ; 8° : pp. 376, [2 maps, 5 engravings.]

CARVER CENTENARY : [See " Collections of the Historical Society."]

EXPLORATORY TRAVELS through the Western Territories of North America: Comprising a voyage from Saint Louis, on the Mississippi, to the source of that river, and a journey through the interior of Louisiana, and the northeastern Provinces of New Spain. Performed in the years 1805, 1806, 1807, by order of the Government of the United States. By Zebulon Montgomery Pike. London: 1811, 4°: pp. 436, [2 maps.]

NARRATIVE JOURNAL OF TRAVELS from Detroit northwest through the Great Chain of American Lakes to the sources of the Mississippi River, in the year 1820. By Henry R. Schoolcraft. Albany: Published by E. & E. Hosford, 1821, 8°: pp. 424. [Map, 7 illustrations.]

NARRATIVE OF AN EXPEDITION to the source of St. Peter's River, Lake Winnipeek, Lake of the Woods, &c. Performed in the Year 1823, by order of the Hon. J. C. Calhoun, Secretary of War, under the Command of Stephen H. Long, U. S. T. E. Compiled from the notes of Major Long, Messrs. Say, Keating & Colhoun, by William II. Keating, A. M. &c., Professor of Mineralogy and Chemistry as applied to the Arts, in the University of Pennsylvania; Geologist and Historiographer to the Expedition. In two Volumes. London: Printed by Geo. B. Whittaker, Ave Maria Lane, 1825, 8°. Vol. 1, Pp. xvi, 458. [4 illustrations and map.] Vol. 2, Pp. vi, 404. [3 illustrations.]

LA DECOUVERTE DES SOURCES DU MISSISSIPPI et de la Riviere Sanglante. Description du Cours entier du Mississippi, Qui n'etait connu, que partiellement, et d'une grand partie de celui de la Riviere Sanglante, presque entierement inconnue; ainsi que du Cours entier de l'Ohio, &c., &c. Coup d'œil, sur les compagnies nord-ouest, et de la baie d' Hudson, ainsi que sur la Colonie Selkirk. Preuves Evidentes, que le Mississippi est la premiere Riviere du Monde. Par J. C. Beltrami, Membre de plusieurs Academies. Nouvelle-Orleans: Imprime par Benj. Levy, No. 86, Rue Royale, 1824. 8°: pp. vii, 328.

A PILGRIMAGE IN EUROPE AND AMERICA, leading to the Discovery of the Sources of the Mississippi and Bloody River; with a description of the whole course of the former, and of the Ohio. By J. C. Beltrami, Esq., formerly Judge of a Royal Court in the Ex-Kingdom of Italy. In two volumes. London: Printed for Hunt and Clarke, York Street, Covent Garden. 1828. 8°. Vol. I, Pp. LXXVI. 472. [2 maps, 1 engraving.] Vol. II, Pp. 546. [1 map, 3 engravings.]

A NARRATIVE OF THE CAPTIVITY AND ADVENTURES OF JOHN TANNER (U. S. Interpreter at the Sault de Ste. Marie,) during Thirty Years' Residence among the Indians in the Interior of North America. Prepared for the Press by Edwin James, M. D., Editor of an account of Major Long's Expedition from Pittsburg to the Rocky Mountains. New York: G. & C. & H. Carvill, 108 Broadway. 1830. 8°: pp. 426. [Portrait of Tanner and numerous wood cuts.]

[Tanner spent a number of years, during his captivity, in Minnesota, and some of his descendants yet live in the State.]

NARRATIVE OF AN EXPEDITION through the Upper Mississippi to Itasca Lake, the actual source of this River; embracing an exploratory trip through the Saint Croix and Burntwood (or Broule) Rivers; in 1832. Under the direction of Henry R. Schoolcraft. New York: Published by Harper & Brothers, No. 82 Cliff Street. 1834. 8°: pages 307. [3 maps.]

SUMMARY NARRATIVE OF AN EXPLORATORY EXPEDITION to the Sources of the Mississippi River, in 1820, resumed and completed by the Discovery of its origin in Itasca Lake, in 1832. By authority of the United States. With appendixes, &c., together with all the Official Reports and Scientific Papers of both Expeditions. By Henry R. Schoolcraft. Philadelphia: Lippincott, Grambo & Co. 1855. 8°: pp. 596. [Maps and Illustrations.]

THE RAMBLER IN NORTH AMERICA, MDCCCXXXII—MDCCCXXXIII. By Charles Joseph Latrobe, author of the "Alpenstock," etc. In two volumes. New York: Published by Harper & Brothers, No. 82, Cliff Street, and' sold by the principal booksellers throughout the United States. 1835. 12°. Vol. 1, Pp. VII, 243. Vol. 2, Pp. 242.

NOTES ON THE WISCONSIN TERRITORY; particularly with reference to the Iowa District, or Black Hawk Purchase. By

3

Lieutenant Albert M. Lea, United States Dragoons. Philadelphia: H. S. Tanner—Shakspeare Buildings. 1836. 24°: [with map:] pp. 53.

A CANOE VOYAGE UP THE MINNAY SOTOR; with an account of the Lead and Copper Deposits in Wisconsin; of the Gold Region in the Cherokee Country; and sketches of popular manners, &c., &c., &c. By G. W. Featherstonhaugh, F. R. S.; F. G. S.; Author of "Excursion through the Slave States." In two Volumes. London: Richard Bentley, New Burlington Street, Publisher in Ordinary to her Majesty. 1847. 8°. Vol. I, Pp. xiv, 416. [6 engravings and map.] Vol. II, Pp. vii, 351. [1 engraving.]

REPORT intended to illustrate a Map of the Hydrographical Basin of the Upper Mississippi River, made by I. N. Nicollet; while in employ under the Bureau of the Corps of Topographical Engineers. January 11, 1845. Washington: Blair & Rives, Printers. 1845. 8°: pp. 170.

PERSONAL MEMOIRS OF A RESIDENCE of Thirty Years with the Indian Tribes on the American Frontiers: with brief notices of passing events, facts, and opinions. A. D. 1812 to A. D. 1842. By Henry R. Schoolcraft. Philadelphia: Lippincott, Grambo and Co., Successors to Grigg, Elliott & Co. 1851. 8°: pp. xlviii, 703.

[This work lacks an index, which greatly impairs its value.]

A SUMMER IN THE WILDERNESS; embracing a Canoe Voyage up the Mississippi and around Lake Superior. By Charles Lanman, author of "Essays for Summer Hours," etc. "And I was in the Wilderness alone."—Bryant. New York: D. Appleton & Company, 200 Broadway, &c. MDCCCXLVII. 12°: pp. 208.

REPORT OF A GEOLOGICAL SURVEY of Wisconsin, Iowa and Minnesota; and incidentally of a portion of Nebraska Territory. Made under instructions from the United States Treasury Department. By David Dale Owen, United States Geologist.

Philadelphia : Lippincott, Grambo & Co. 1852. 4° : pp. 638. [72 wood cuts ; 27 steel plates ; 18 colored maps, stone and copper.]

*** All the above are strictly Minnesota books—the authors of them having travelled in some portion of the State, as it now is. In addition to these, the student of Minnesota history should consult DuPratz, Charlevoix, the N. Y. Colonial Documents, &c., for incidental references to the region now known as Minnesota.

MINNESOTA: HISTORICAL, DESCRIPTIVE AND STATISTICAL.

THE HOMES OF THE NEW WORLD ; Impressions of America. By Frederika Bremer. Translated by Mary Howitt. "Sing unto the Lord a new Song."—*Psalm* xcvi. In two volumes. New York : Harper & Brothers, Publishers, 329 and 331, Pearl street, Franklin Square. 1864. 12°. Vol. I, Pp. xii, 651. Vol. II, 654.

[Miss Bremer visited Minnesota in 1849; sixty-three pages of the 2d .Vol. are devoted to it.]

SKETCHES OF MINNESOTA, the New England of the West. With Incidents of Travel in that Territory during the Summer of 1849. In two Parts. By E. S. Seymour. With a Map. New York : Harper & Brothers, Publishers, 82 Cliff street. 1850. 12° : pp. 281. [Map.]

[Mr. Seymour lived at Galena, and made a short trip through Minnesota in 1849. His work is interesting and well written, and for three or four years was the only work descriptive of Minnesota accessible to the public. He is said to have died in 1852.]

REPORT OF THE SECRETARY OF WAR, communicating the report of an Exploration of the Territory of Minnesota, by Brevet Captain Pope. March 21, 1850. 8° : pp. 56.

[Ex. Doc. No. 42. 31st Congress, 1st Session.]

PEMBINA SETTLEMENT. Letter from the Secretary of War, transmitting report of Maj. Wood, relative to his Expedition to Pembina Settlement, and the condition of affairs on the North-Western frontier of the Territory of Minnesota. March 19, 1850. 8° : pp. 55.

[Ex. Doc. No. 51 : 31st Congress, 1st Session.]

MINNESOTA YEAR BOOK FOR 1851, by W. G. Le Duc. Published by W. G. Le Duc, Bookseller and Stationer, St. Paul, Minnesota Territory. 12°: pp. 51.

—— do, for 1852 : 12°: pp. 98 : [cut.]

—— do, for 1853 : 12°: pp. 37: [map.]

MINNESOTA AND ITS RESOURCES, to which are appended Camp-fire Sketches, or Notes of a Trip from Saint Paul to Pembina and Selkirk Settlement on the Red River of the North. By J. Wesley Bond. Redfield, 110 and 112, Nassau Street, New York. 1853. 12°: pp. 364. [Map, and numerous illustrations.]

Do. do. Tenth (?) Edition. Keen & Lee, No. 148 Lake Street, Chicago, Illinois. Charles Desilver, No. 253, Market Street, Philadelphia. 1856. [Map and numerous illustrations.] Pp. 412.

[The back is titled "Minnesota as it Is."]

SURVEY, etc., of Road from Mendota to Big Sioux River. Letter from the Secretary of War, transmitting Report of the Survey, &c., of road from Mendota to the Big Sioux River. By Capt. J. L. Reno, U. S. A. April 28, 1854. 8°: pp. 12.

[Ex. Doc. No. 97: 33d Congress, 1st Session.]

THE MINNESOTA MESSENGER, containing Sketches of the Rise and Progress of Minnesota; Tables of Distances from Different Points; Directions to Strangers; and various other Information, invaluable to the Traveller and Business Man. Saint Paul, M. T. A. D. Munson, Editor and Publisher. 1855. 8°: pp. 78.

RISE AND PROGRESS OF MINNESOTA TERRITORY, Including a Statement of the Business Prosperity of Saint Paul; and Information in Regard to the Different Counties, Cities, Towns and Villages in the Territory, Etc. St. Paul: Published by C. L. Emerson, Minnesota Democrat Office, 1855. Royal 8°: pp. 64.

MINNESOTA AND THE FAR WEST, by Laurence Oliphant, Esq., Late Civil Secretary and Superintendent-General of Indian Affairs in Canada. Author of "The Russian Shores of the Black Sea," &c. William Blackwood and Sons, Edinburgh and London. MDCCCLV. 8°: pp. XIV, 306. [Map; 13 illustrations.]

[Originally published in Blackwood's Magazine.]

THE IMMIGRANT'S GUIDE TO MINNESOTA IN 1856. By an Old Resident. St. Anthony: W. W. Wales, Bookseller and Publisher. 12°: pp. 116. [5 wood cuts.]

THE MINNESOTA HANDBOOK, for 1856-7. With a new and accurate map. By Nathan H. Parker, author of "Iowa as it Is," &c. Boston: John P. Jewett and Company. MDCCCLVII. 12°: pp. 159. [Map.]

MINNESOTA AND DACOTAH: In letters descriptive of a Tour through the Northwest, in the Autumn of 1856. With Information Relative to Public Lands, and a Table of Statistics. By C. C. Andrews, Counsellor at Law; Editor of the Official Opinions of the Attorneys General of the United States. Washington: Robert Farnham. 1857. 12°: pp. 215.

FLORAL HOME; or, First Years of Minnesota. Early Sketches, Later Settlements, and Further Developments. By Harriet E. Bishop. New York: Sheldon, Blakeman & Company. 1857. 12°: pp. 342. [Portrait of Author, and numerous Illustrations.]

MINNESOTA: Address delivered at the Broadway House, New York, on the 27th March, 1857, by Ignatius Donnelly, Esq. New York: Folger & Turner, Printers, No. 118 John Street. 1857. 12°: pp. 16.

A GUIDE TO EMIGRANTS TO MINNESOTA. By a Tourist. St. Paul: Goodrich, Somers & Co., Printers. 1857. 12°: pp. 23.

THE EMIGRANT'S GUIDE to Iowa, Wisconsin and Minnesota. Containing a Correct History of all the Towns on the Mississippi River and its Tributaries, from Dubuque to its Head Waters. Also, all the Principal Towns in Minnesota. Published by J. Q. A. Ward, and M. V. B. Young, St. Paul. Printed at the Minnesotian Office. 1857. 24°: pp. 184.

THE HISTORY OF MINNESOTA: From the Earliest French Explorations, to the present time. By Edward Duffield Neill, Secretary of the Minnesota Historical Society. "Nec falsa *dicere, rec vera reticere."* Philadelphia: J. B. Lippincott & Co. 1858. 8°: pp. 628. [4 maps.]

—— Do. do. Large Paper Copy; with 36 steel engravings illustrating Indian Life, 8 steel portraits and 5 maps.

MINNESOTA: or "A Bundle of Facts," going to Illustrate its Great Past, the Grand Present, and her Glorious Future; by a Southern Pre-Emptor. [*Thomas B. Winston.*] 5,000 copies issued for gratuitous circulation. New Orleans: Published by J. B. Steel, No. 60 Camp Street. 1858. 24°: pp. 32.

MINNESOTA: Its Place among the States. Being the First Annual Report of the Commissioner of Statistics, for the Year ending Jan. 1, 1860. Published by authority of law. Hartford: Press of Case, Lockwood and Company. 1860. 8°: pp. 174.

MINNESOTA: Its Progress and Capabilities. Being the Second Annual Report of the Commissioner of Statistics, for the Years 1860 and 1861. Saint Paul: Wm. R. Marshall, State Printer. 1862. 8°: pp. 127.

[Joseph A. Wheelock was Commissioner of Statistics, 1860-63.]

STATISTICS OF MINNESOTA, pertaining to its Agriculture, Population, Manufactures, etc., etc., for 1869. Being the First Annual Report of the Assistant Secretary of State [*Pennock Pusey*] to the Governor. Made according to law. Saint Paul: Press Printing Co. 1870. 8°: pp. 152.

EMIGRATION, with special reference to Minnesota, U. S. and British Columbia. By Thomas Rawlings. London: Clayton & Co., Printers. 8°: pp. 24. Map. [1864.]

NOTES UPON THE GEOLOGY of some portions of Minnesota, from St. Paul to the Western Part of the State. By James Hall. 1866. 4°: pp. 12.

GEOLOGY AND MINERALS. A Report of Explorations in the Mineral Regions of Minnesota during the Years 1848, 1859 and 1864, by Col. Charles Whittlesey. Printed by order of the General Assembly [*of Minnesota*]. Cleveland: Herald Office. 1866. 8°: pp. 54.

MINNESOTA AS A HOME FOR IMMIGRANTS. Being the First

and Second Prize Essays awarded by the Board of Examiners appointed Pursuant to an Act of the Legislature of the State of Minnesota. Approved March 4, 1864. St. Paul: Pioneer Printing Company. 1866. 8°: pp. 84.

[I. Mary J. Colburn. II. W. R. Smith.]

HAND BOOK OF MINNESOTA: Describing its Agricultural, Commercial and Manufacturing Resources, and other Capabilities of Producing Wealth; also, its Physical and Social Conditions and Its Future. By Rufus Blanchard. Chicago: Blanchard & Cram. 1867. 18°: pp. 64.

TOURISTS AND INVALID'S GUIDE TO THE NORTHWEST. Containing Information about Minnesota, Wisconsin, Dacota, and the Lake Superior Region. Compiled by Charles H. Sweetser, New York. 1867. 8°: pp. 50.

UPPER MISSISSIPPI; or, Historical Sketches of the Mound Builders, the Indian Tribes, and the Progress of Civilization in the Northwest; from A. D. 1600 to the Present Time. By George Gale. Chicago: Clarke and Company. 1867. 12°: pp. 460. [With portrait of Author.]

MINNESOTA: Its Advantages to Settlers. Being a brief Synopsis of its History and Progress, Climate, Soil, Agricultural and Manufacturing Facilities, and Social Status; Its Lakes, Rivers and Railroads; Homestead and Exemption Laws; Embracing a concise Treatise on its Climatology, in a Hygienic and Sanitary Point of View; Its unparalleled Salubrity, Growth and Productiveness, as compared with the Older States, and the elements of its Future Greatness and Prosperity. For Gratuitous Circulation. Order Copies to any Address, from Girart Hewitt, St. Paul, Minn. 1867. 8°: pp. 36.

[This is usually called "Hewitt's Pamphlet." 150,000 copies of this have been issued.]

TOURIST'S GUIDE TO THE UPPER MISSISSIPPI RIVER: Giving all the Railroad and Steamboat Routes Diverging from Chicago, Milwaukee & Dubuque toward Saint Paul, etc. Compiled by J. Disturnell. New York. 1868. 12°: pp. 92. [Maps.]

DAKOTA LAND; or the Beauty of Saint Paul. An Original, Illustrated, Historic and Romantic Work, presenting a Combination of Marvellous Dreams and Wandering Fancies, Singular Events and Strange Fatalities, all interwoven with Graphic Descriptions of the Beautiful Scenery and Wonderful Enchantment in Minnesota. To which is added "A Round of Pleasure," with interesting Notes of Travel, Maps, etc., and Forming a Comprehensive Guide to the Great North West. By Col. Hankins, Editor of "The New York Home Gazette," &c. 1868: Hankins & Son, Publishers, New York. 12°: pp. 460. [Illustrations and Map.]

ADDRESS OF THE MINNESOTA IRISH EMIGRATION CONVENTION, held in the City of Saint Paul, Minnesota, Jan. 20, 1869, to the People of Ireland. Saint Paul: North Western Chronicle Print. 1869. 8°: pp. 22.

THE MINNESOTA GUIDE. A Hand Book of Information for the Traveller, Pleasure Seekers & Immigrants, concerning all Routes of Travel to and in the State; Sketches of the Towns and Cities in the Same, etc., etc. [By J. F. Williams.] Saint Paul: E. H. Burritt & Co. 1869. 16°: pp. 100. [9 cuts, 1 map.]

MINNESOTA AS IT IS IN 1870. Its General Resources and Attractions * * * with special descriptions of all its Counties and Towns. * * * By J. W. McClung. St. Paul: Published by the Author. 1870. 12°: pp. 300. [Map.]

THE SEAT OF EMPIRE. By Charles Carleton Coffin. ("Carleton.") Boston: Fields, Osgood & Co. 1870. 12°: pp. 232. [Map;. 6 engravings.]

MINNESOTA GAZETTEER AND BUSINESS DIRECTORY.—See "State Gazetteers and Directories."

EDWARDS' DESCRIPTIVE GAZETTEER OF THE MISSISSIPPI RIVER. —See do. do.

THE SIOUX WAR OF 1862–3. See "The Indian Tribes of Minnesota."

EMIGRATION DOCUMENTS, IN EUROPEAN LANGUAGES.

NACHRICHTEN UBER MINNESOTA. Gesammelt von Eduard Pelz. Hamburg, 1858. 8° : pp. 25.

UEBER AUSWANDERUNG. Von Ed. Pelz. Besonderer Abdruck aus der " Deutschen Auswanderer—Ztg." No. 47-49. Bremen, 1864. 12° : pp. 25.

DIE AUSWANDERUNG MIT BESONDERER BEZIEHUNG AUF MINNESOTA UND BRITISH COLUMBIA. Von Thomas Rawlings. Aus dem Englishen ubertragen und eingeleitet, von Eduard Pelz. Hamburg : Hoffman & Campe, 1866. 12° : pp. 63.

MINNESOTA IN SEINEN HAUPTVERHALTNISSEN. Emigrations-Monographie von Eduard Pelz. Dritte Auflage. Hamburg : Hoffman & Campe. 1866. 8° : pp. 52.

MINNESOTA OG DETS FORDELE FOR INVANDREREN, &c. Uddeles gratis. La Crosse, Wis. Trykt : Fadrelandets Officin. 1867. 12° : pp. 30. [Written by Hon. H. Mattson,]

MINNESOTA OCH DESS FORDELAR FOR INVANDRAREN ; &c. Utdelas Gratis. Chicago : Svenska Amerikanarens Boktryckeri, 1867. 12° : pp. 29. [By H. Mattson.]

MINNESOTA, (Vereenigde Staten von Nord-Amerika) in zijne Hulpbronnen, Vruchtbaarheid en Ontwikkeling Geschetst, voor Landverhuizers en Kapitalisten door J. H. Kloos, ingenieur. Amsterdam : H. de Hoogh. 1867. 8° : pp. 54. Another Edition. With Map. pp. 61.

INLICHTINGEN OMTRENT DEN ST. PAUL EN PACIFIC-SPOORWEG, medegedeeld door W. v. O. B. Schriver van " Amerikaanische Fondsen als Geldbelegging." Amsterdam : H. de Hoogh. 1868. 8° : pp. 20.

MINNESOTA DAS CENTRAL-GEBIET NORD AMERICAS. In seinen Hauptverhaltnissen dargestellt, von Eduard Pelz. Leipzig : Verlagsbuchandlung von J. J. Weber. 1868. 8° : pp. 31.

STATEN MINNESOTA ; Nordamerika. Dens Fordele for den Skandinaviske Invandrer med saerligt hensyn til jordbrugeren. Af Soren Listol, Medredaktor af " Nordisk Folkblad." 1869-70.

4

Udgivet for Statens Regning. Uddeles Gratis. Nordisk Folkeblad Officin, Minneapolis. 1869. 12°: pp. 25.

MINNESOTA ALS EINE HEIMAT FUR EINWANDERER. Dritte Jahresausgabe, publizirt in Auftrage des Staates. St. Paul, Minn. 1869. Staats-Zeitung Officin. 8°: pp. 40.

TOWN AND COUNTY HISTORIES.

AN ADDRESS giving the Early History of Hennepin County delivered before the Minneapolis Lyceum, by Col. John H. Stevens, and published by Order of the Lyceum. Minneapolis: Printed at the North-Western Democrat Office. 1856. 8°: pp. 12.

OPINION AND DECISION of Hon. A. G. Chatfield, between adverse claimants to lands in the Town site of Hastings. St. Paul. 1857. 8°: pp. 20.

ADVANTAGES AND RESOURCES of Houston County, Minnesota. Hokah, Minn. Published by Reynolds and Wertz. Printed at the Hokah Chief Office. 1858. 18°: pp. 34.

HISTORY OF FILLMORE COUNTY, MINNESOTA, with an outline of her Resources, Advantages, and the Inducements she offers to those seeking Homes in the West. By J. W. Bishop, C. E. Chatfield, Minn.: Holly & Brown, Printers, Republican Office. 1858. 12°: pp. 40. [Map.]

CITY OF WINONA AND SOUTHERN MINNESOTA: a Sketch of their Growth and Prospects, with General Information for the Emigrant, Mechanic, Farmer and Capitalist. D. Sinclair & Co., Publishers. 1858. 8°: pp. 36.

SCHOOL LAW: with the Rules and Regulations of the Board of Education of the City of St. Anthony. Thomas & Clark, Printers, St. Anthony. 1860. 12°: pp. 15.

THE CHARTER AND AMENDMENTS THERETO, AND ORDINANCES OF THE CITY OF ST. ANTHONY. Printed and published by authority of the Corporation. Thomas & Clark, City Printers. 1861.

COMMERCIAL ADVERTISER DIRECTORY, for Saint Anthony and Minneapolis; to which is added a Business Directory. 1859-1860. H. E. Chamberlain, Publisher. Saint Anthony & Minneapolis. Printed by Croffut & Clarke, News Office. 1859. 8°: pp. 162.

SUMMARY STATEMENT of the General Interests of Manufacture and Trade connected with the Upper Mississippi. By Hon. David Heaton. Together with the Hydrographical Survey and Geology of the Mississippi River from Fort Snelling to St. Anthony Falls, by T. M. Griffith and Dr. C. L. Anderson. Published by the Board of Trade of Minneapolis and St. Anthony. 1862. 8°: pp. 12.

MINNEAPOLIS DIRECTORY, for the years 1865-6, comprising a complete Directory of citizens and business firms, a classified Business Directory, and city and county Register. Price, $2. Minneapolis: E. P. Shaw, Publisher. 1865. 8°: pp. 99.

WINONA DIRECTORY for 1866-67: Comprising a Complete List of all residents in the City; City and County Officers, Churches, Public Schools, etc. Compiled by John M. Wolfe, Winona. A. Bailey, Publisher. 1866. 8°: pp. 124.

GEOGRAPHICAL AND STATISTICAL HISTORY OF THE COUNTY OF OLMSTED, together with a general view of the State of Minnesota, from its Earliest Settlement to the present time. By W. H. Mitchell. Rochester, Minn.: Shaver & Eaton, Printers. 1866. 16°: pp. 121.

HISTORY AND BUSINESS DIRECTORY OF WRIGHT COUNTY. Classified by Towns. Containing a Correct and Concise History of Each Town and Village in the County, together with a Classified List of all Business Houses, Statistics of Population, Wealth, Increase, Crops, &c. Published by George Gray, Statesman Office, Monticello, Minn. 1867. 16°: pp. 32.

MANKATO AND BLUE EARTH COUNTY. A Brief Review of the Past, Present and Future of the City, together with its Geographical and Commercial Position, its Schools, Churches, Public Halls, Assessed Valuation and Rapid Growth in 1866, &c., &c. By Wm. B. Griswold, Editor Mankato Union. Printed by Griswold & Neff, Union Office. 1867. 12°: pp. 20.

A VIEW OF ST. ANTHONY FALLS, Present and Prospective : being a Report of the Manufacturing, Commercial and General Advantages of St. Anthony Falls, Minnesota. By W. D. Storey. Minneapolis : Atlas Printing House. 1867. 8° : pp. 37.

WASECA COUNTY in Minnesota, as a Home for Immigrants. By Jas. E. Child. Published and for sale at the Wilton Weekly News Office, Wilton, Minn. 1867. 18° : pp. 52.

GEOGRAPHICAL AND STATISTICAL HISTORY OF STEELE COUNTY, from its Earliest Settlement to the Present Time ; Embracing Leading Incidents of Pioneer Life, Names of Early Settlers, Nature of Soil, Advantages to Settlers, &c., &c. By W. H. Mitchell. Minneapolis : Tribune Printing Company. 1868. 16° : pp. 97.

DAKOTA COUNTY. Its Past and Present, Geographical, Statistical and Historical, together with a General View of the State ; by W. H. Mitchell. Tribune Printing Company, Minneapolis. 1868. 16° : pp. 162. [Steel plate of Gen. Sibley and six wood cuts.]

GEOGRAPHICAL AND STATISTICAL HISTORY OF THE COUNTY OF HENNEPIN, embracing Leading Incidents in Pioneer Life, the Names of the Early Settlers, and the Progress in Wealth and Population to the Present Time. By W. H. Mitchell and J. H. Stevens. Minneapolis : Russell & Belfoy, Printers. 1868. 16° : pp. 149.

A RECORD OF RICE COUNTY, Minn., in 1868, being a Review of the Settlement, Growth and Prosperity of the County, and a Brief Description of its Towns and Villages. By F. W. Frink. Faribault : Printed at the Central Republican Office. 1868. 12° : pp. 24.

BLUE EARTH COUNTY : Its Advantages to Settlers. A Description of its History, Progress, Climate, Soil, Agricultural, Manufacturing & Commercial Facilities. To which is added a Brief Description of the Other Counties of Southwestern Minnesota. By J. A. Willard, of Mankato. Published by J. C. Wise, " Record" Office, Mankato, Minn. 1868. 8° : pp. 20.

THE WATER POWER OF THE FALLS OF ST. ANTHONY. 1868. Third Annual Report of Manufacturing Industry at the Cities of Minneapolis and St. Anthony, Minnesota, &c. Minneapolis. 1869. 8°: pp. 16.

FARIBAULT COUNTY, MINNESOTA: Its History, Towns, Climate, Improvements, Villages, Civil, Religious, Moral and Educational Institutions, &c., &c. [No imprint.] 12°: pp. 24. [1868?]

SUPREME COURT: January Term, 1868. Village of Mankato, Respondent, vs. Jno. A. Willard and Sheldon T. Barney, Appellants, &c., &c. 12°: pp. 38.

[Supreme Court brief, containing quite a full account of the early settlement of Mankato.]

BOARD OF TRADE OF THE CITY OF MANKATO. Articles of Corporation, By-Laws, Officers, Committees and Members. Organized Sept. 16, 1868. Mankato, Minnesota. 'Mankato Union Print. 1869. 8°: pp. 14.

CAPT. P. B. DAVY's EXPEDITION. Printed April, 1868, at Blue Earth City, Minn., in the Office of the "South West." 12°: pp. 24.

[Most of it is a Sketch of Blue Earth City.]

RULES AND REGULATIONS for the government of the Public Schools in the City of Red Wing, Minnesota. 1869. Argus Printing House. 1869.

SALE OF FORT SNELLING RESERVATION. Letter from the Secretary of War, transmitting Papers Relative to the Sale of the Fort Snelling Reservation. Dec. 10, 1868. 8°: pp. 107.

[Ex. Doc. No. 9. 40th Congress, 3d Session; H. of R. Contains a valuable Documentary History of Fort Snelling, and other historical facts.]

STRANGERS' GUIDE in Minneapolis and Surrounding Country. With a complete and accurate description of all Places and Objects of Interest to Tourists, Artists, Sportsmen, &c. Tables of Distances, Statistics, &c. Prepared by a Resident [Newton H. Chittenden?] Minneapolis: Tribune Printing Company. 1869. 16°: pp. 40.

GEOGRAPHICAL AND STATISTICAL SKETCH of the Past and Present of Goodhue County, together with a general view of

the State of Minnesota.   By W. H. Mitchell, Minneapolis :
O. S. King's Book and Job Printing House.   1869.   16° :
pp. 191.   [4 wood cuts.]

REPORT of the Select Committee to which was referred that
part of the Message of the Governor of Minnesota relating to
Duluth, as a Harbor and Port of Entry.   Saint Paul : Pioneer
Printing Company.   1870.   8° : pp. 21.   [Map.]

MANKATO—Dedication of First Presb. Church : see " Sermons," &c.

MINNEAPOLIS—Westminster Presby. Church.   Do.   do.
——   Parish Manual of Gethsemane Church : see
          " Churches."

SAINT PAUL—Institution of the Masonic Order : see " Masonic."
——   Catalogues of Baldwin School and Female
          Seminary : see " Catalogues," &c.

SAINT ANTHONY—Catalogues of Sigourney Boarding School
and State University.   Do.   do.

RED WING—Catalogues of Hamline University.
——   Manual of First Presbyterian Church of :
          see " Churches," &c.
——   Stone Heaps at : see Vol. I, Histor. Soc. Coll.

FARIBAULT—Catalogues of St. Mary's Hall, &c. : see " Catalogues."
——   Bishop Seabury Mission : see " Churches."

NORTHFIELD—Do. of Northfield College : see " Catalogues."

WASIOJA—Do. of Minnesota Seminary.   Do.   do.

FORT SNELLING—See Mrs. Eastman's " Dahcotah."
——   List of early Steamboat Arrivals at : see Vol. I,
          Histor. Soc. Collections.
——   Occurrences from 1819 to 1840 : see Vol. II. Do.

STATE GAZETTEERS AND "DIRECTORIES."

MINNESOTA GAZETTEER, and Business Directory for 1865. Containing a List of Cities, Villages and Post Offices in the State; a list of Business Firms, etc., etc. With much other Useful Information. Saint Paul: Groff & Bailey, Publishers. 1865. 8°: pp. 399.

MERWIN'S BUSINESS DIRECTORY OF MINNESOTA, for 1869-70. Containing a Classified List, Alphabetically Arranged by Towns, of Business Firms, Manufacturing Establishments, etc., etc. Saint Paul: Heman Merwin, Publisher. 1869. 8°: pp. 308.

EDWARD'S DESCRIPTIVE GAZETTEER AND COMMERCIAL DIRECTORY OF THE MISSISSIPPI RIVER, from Saint Cloud to New Orleans, embracing Historical and Descriptive Sketches of all the Cities, Towns and Villages, etc., etc. Published by Edwards, Greenough & Deved, St. Louis. 1866. 8°: pp. 1170. [Maps and numerous cuts.]

RELATIONS OF MINNESOTA TO THE NORTHWEST.

SPEECH OF THE HON. WM. H. NOBLES, together with Other Documents, relative to an Emigrant Route to California and Oregon, through Minnesota Territory. Printed by Order of the House of Representatives. Saint Paul: Olmsted & Brown, Territorial Printers. 1854. 8°: pp. 13.

REPORT from a Select Committee of the House of Representatives, on the Overland Emigration Route from Minnesota to British Oregon. With an Appendix. Printed by order of the H. of R. St. Paul: Earle S. Goodrich, State Printer. 1858. 8°: pp. 100.

PROCEEDINGS of a Public Meeting of Citizens of Minnesota, in favor of a Semi-Weekly Overland Mail from Saint Paul to Puget Sound. Held Jan. 3, 1859. Saint Paul: Pioneer Printing Company. 1859. 8°: pp. 16.

MEMORIAL of the Chamber of Commerce of Saint Paul, rela-

tive to the Navigation of the Red River of the North.
Presented to the House of Representatives, Feb. 10, 1859, by
the Hon. James M. Cavanaugh, of Minnesota. Washington,
1859. 8°: pp. 15.

THE NEW NORTH WEST. By [*Rev.*] Burdett Hart, Fair
Haven, Conn. [From the New Englander for Nov., 1859.]
8°: pp. 21.

NORTH-WEST BRITISH AMERICA, and Its Relations to the
State of Minnesota. By James W. Taylor. Printed as a
Supplement to the Journal of the House of Representatives,
Session of 1859-60. St. Paul: Newson, Moore, Foster & Co.,
Printers. 1860. 8°: pp. 53.
—— Do. Do. Another edition, from type of the " Minne-
sotian & Times." March 3, 1860. [With map.]

RELATIONS between the United States and North-West British
America. Letter from the Secretary of the Treasury, in answer
to a Resolution of the House of 20th May last, &c. [Exec.
Doc. No. 146: 37th Congress, 2d Session.] 8°: pp. 85. July
11, 1862.

IDAHO: her Gold Fields, and the Routes to them. A Hand
Book for Emigrants. By Capt. Jas. L. Fisk, A. Q. M. 1863.
New York: John A. Gray, Printer. 18°: pp. 99. [Map.]
[Reprint of the foregoing.]

EXPEDITION OF CAPT. FISK TO THE ROCKY MOUNTAINS. Letter from the Secretary of War in answer to a resolution of the
House of Feb. 26. Transmitting report of Captain Fisk of his
late expedition to the Rocky Mountains and Idaho. 8°: pp. 39.
[March 3, 1864. Ex. Doc. No. 45: 88th Congress, 1st Session.]

CAPT. FISK'S FOURTH EXPEDITION from Saint Cloud, Minnesota, to the Great Gold Fields of Montana, &c. 3d edition.
St. Paul: Press Printing Company. 1866. 12°: pp. 12.

[THE WINNIPEG REBELLION:] Message of the President of
the U. S. communicating, in compliance with a resolution of
the Senate, information, &c. Feb. 3, 1870. [Ex. Doc. No.
33.] 8°: pp. 52.

MINNESOTA AND THE FAR WEST.—See "Historical, Descriptive," &c.

MINNESOTA AND DACOTAH.— Do. do.

EMIGRANT'S GUIDE to Iowa, Wisconsin and Minnesota.— Do.

TOURIST'S AND INVALID'S GUIDE to the North West.— Do.

HYDROGRAPHY OF THE UPPER MISSISSIPPI.

SURVEY OF UPPER MISSISSIPPI RIVER. . Letter from the Secretary of War, in answer to a resolution of the House * * * with General Warren's report of the Surveys of the Upper Mississippi River and its Tributaries. 8°: pp. 116.
[Senate Doc.: 39th Congress, 2d Session. Feb. 15, 1867.]

—— Do. Report of Gen. Warren for year ending June 30, 1867. 8°: pp. 6.
["Appendix D;" Report of the Chief of Engineers. Ex. Doc. No. 1; H. of R.; 40th Congress, 2d Session. Dated Sept. 14, 1867.]

—— Do. Letter from the Secretary of War, transmitting General Warren's report of a Survey of the Upper Mississippi River. 8°: pp. 10.
[Ex. Doc. No. 247: 40th Congress, 2d Session. April 8, 1868.]

—— Do. Report of Gen. Warren for Year ending June 30, 1868. 8°: pp. 86.
["Appendix G;" Report of the Chief of Engineers. Ex. Doc. I, Part 2: H. of R.; 40th Congress, 3d Session. Dated Aug. 31, 1868.]

"CERTAIN PHYSICAL FEATURES OF THE UPPER MISSISSIPPI RIVER." A paper read by Gen. G. K. Warren before the American Association for the Advancement of Science; Chicago, Ill. Aug. 5–12, 1868, 8°: pp. 6.

NICOLLET'S REPORT on the Hydrography of the Upper Mississippi.—See "Early Explorations and Travels."

EDWARD'S DIRECTORY OF THE MISSISSIPPI RIVER.—See "Gazetteers," &c.

HYDROGRAPHICAL SURVEY OF THE MISSISSIPPI, between Fort
5

Snelling and St. Anthony Falls.—See "Town and County History."

THE WATER POWER OF THE FALLS OF ST. ANTHONY.—See do.

MEMOIR ON THE PHYSICAL GEOGRAPHY OF MINNESOTA.—See Vol. I, Hist. Soc. Collec.

THE INDIAN TRIBES OF MINNESOTA.

DAHCOTAH; or Life and Legends of the Sioux around Fort Snelling. By Mrs. Mary Eastman; with preface by Mrs. C. M. Kirkland. Illustrated from drawings by Capt. Eastman. New York: John Wiley, 161 Broadway. 1849. 12°. Pp. XIII, 268.

THE ROMANCE OF INDIAN LIFE. By Mrs. Mary H. Eastman. With other tales, Selections from the Iris, an illuminated Souvenir. Philadelphia: Lippincott, Grambo & Co. 1853. 8°. Pp. VI, 298. [10 illustrations.]

[Mrs. Eastman now resides in Washington City, D. C.]

LETTERS AND NOTES on the Manners, Customs, and Condition of the North American Indians. Written during eight years' Travel amongst the wildest Tribes of Indians in North America; by Geo. Catlin. In two volumes, with 150 illustrations, &c. Philadelphia: Willis P. Hazard. 1857. Pp. 792.

DAHKOTAH LAND AND DAHKOTAH LIFE, with the History of the Fur Traders of the extreme Northwest during the French and British Dominions. By Edw. D. Neill. Philadelphia: Lippincott & Co. 1859. 8°: pp. 239.

[This is a reprint of a portion of Neill's History of Minnesota.]

THE SIOUX WAR: What has been done by the Minnesota Campaign of 1863: What should be done during a Dakota Campaign of 1864, Etc. By James W. Taylor. Saint Paul: Press Printing Co. 1863. 8°: pp. 16.

HISTORY OF THE SIOUX WAR and Massacres of 1862 and 1863; by Isaac V. D. Heard. With Portraits and Illustrations. New York: Harper & Brothers. 1864. 8°: pp. 354. [33 engravings.]

Mrs. Eastlick's Narrative [*of Captivity among the Sioux*] 1863. 12°: pp. 37.

Dakota War Whoop; or Indian Massacres and War in Minnesota. By Harriet E. Bishop McConkey. Saint Paul: Published by D. D. Merrill. Press Printing Company. 1863. 12°: pp. 304.

Dakota War Whoop: or, Indian Massacres and War in Minnesota, of 1862–'3. By Harriet E. Bishop McConkey, Author of "Floral Homes," &c. Revised Edition. Saint Paul: Published for the Author. Wm. J. Moses' Press, Auburn, N. Y. 1864. 12°: pp. 429.

Miss Coleson's Narrative of her Captivity Among the Sioux Indians! An Interesting and Remarkable Account of the Terrible Sufferings and Providential Escape of Miss Ann Coleson, a Victim of the late Indian Outrages in Minnesota. Philadelphia: Published by Barclay & Co. 1864. 8°: pp. 70. [Several illustrations.]

Six Weeks in the Sioux Tepees: a Narrative of Indian Captivity, by Mrs. Sarah F. Wakefield. Second Edition. Shakopee: Argus Printing Office. 1864. 12°: pp. 63.

A History of the Great Massacre by the Sioux Indians, in Minnesota, including the personal narratives of many who escaped. By Charles S. Bryant, A. M. and Abel B. Murch. (8th thousand.) Cincinnati: Rickey and Carroll, Publishers. 1864. 12°: pp. 504. [7 illustrations.]

Effort & Failure to Civilize the Aborigines. Letter to Hon. N. G. Taylor, Commissioner of Indian Affairs, from Edward D. Neill, late Secretary Minnesota Historical Society. Washington: Government Printing Office. 1868.

Taopi and His Friends; or the Indian's Wrongs and Rights. Philadelphia: Claxton, Remsen and Haffelfinger. 1869. 12°. Pp. xviii, 125. [*With portrait of Taopi.*]

White and Red; a Narrative of Life among the North West Indians; by Helen C. Weeks. With 8 illustrations by A. P. Close. N. Y. Published by Hurd & Houghton. 1869. 12°: pp. 266.

[Originally printed in the Riverside Magazine.]

TAH-KOO WAH-KAN; or, the Gospel among the Dakotas; by
Stephen R. Riggs, A. M., Missionary of the A. B. C. F. M.
and author of the Dakota Grammar & Dictionary. With an
Introduction by S. B. Treat, Secretary of the A. B. C. F. M.
Boston: Cong. Sabbath-School and Publishing Society. 1869.
12°: pp. 491. [3 illustrations.]

REMINISCENCES OF HOLE-IN-THE-DAY (Elder and Younger;)
Julius T. Clark; and Rev. A. Brunson. Wisconsin Historical
Collections. Vol. V, pages 378–409. [Madison. 1869. 8°.]

HISTORICAL AND STATISTICAL INFORMATION Respecting the
History, Condition and Prospects of the Indian Tribes of the
United States: Collected and prepared by Henry R. Schoolcraft,
LL. D. Illustrated by Seth Eastman, Capt. U. S. A. Pub-
lished by Authority of Congress. Philadelphia: Lippincott,
Grambo & Co. 1851–1857. 4°.

[This magnificent work contains hundreds of references, *passim*, to Minnesota and her Indian Tribes, while the illustrations of Capt. Eastman almost
wholly refer to this State, its Indian population, and its scenery. The fol-
owing papers relate entirely to Minnesota:]

VOL. I. Geographical Memoranda respecting the Discovery of the Mississippi River, with a Map of its Source, pp. 133–149; Minnesota, pp.
181–192; Dacotahs of the Mississippi, by Dr. Thos. S. Williamson,
pp. 247–256; Census of Dakotahs, p. 498.

VOL. II. The Dacotah Tribe, p. 37; Natural Caves in the Mississippi
River banks in the Sioux Country, by I. N. Nicollet, p. 95.

VOL. III. Sioux, or Dakota proper, by P. Prescott, pp. 225–247; The Gods
of the Dakotas, by Capt. S. Eastman, p. 485; The Giant's Feast and
Dance, do. p. 487; Indian Population of the Upper Mississippi,
1806, by Lieut. Z. M. Pike, pp. 562–570; Sioux Population in 1836, pp.
612–615.

VOL. IV. Manners, Customs, and Opinions of the Dakotas, by P. Prescott, pp. 59–72; Demoniacal Observances of the Dakotahs, by Capt.
Eastman, pp. 495–501; Bibliography of Dakota Books, p. 546; Power
and Influence of Dakota Medicine Men, by Rev. G. H. Pond, pp.
635–655.

VOL. V. Education among the Dakotas, by Rev. S. R. Riggs, pp. 695–698;
Sioux Population of the Seven Tribes in 1851, by P. Prescott, p. 101.

VOL. VI. War between the Chippewa and Sioux, p. 387; Cession of Territory in Minnesota by the Chippewas, p. 482; Religion and Mytho-
logical Opinions of the Mississippi Valley Tribes, p. 647.

"The Mound Builders, &c." By Geo. Gale.—See "Historical, Descriptive," &c.

Perrot—Mœurs, Coutumes, Religion, &c., des Sauvages.—
See " Early Explorations," &c.

Hennepin—   do.

La Hontan—   do.

Carver's Travels.—See " Early Explorations," &c.

Tanner's Narrative of Captivity.—   do.

Schoolcraft—" Personal Memoirs." etc.   do.

DAKOTA BIBLIOGRAPHY.

In preparing this list of Dakota works, (all of which were written in
Minnesota, for missions located in this State, and a number of which were
also printed here,) I must acknowledge my obligation to Rev. S. R. Riggs,
now of Ft. Wadsworth, D. T., who kindly revised the list, adding interesting
notes, and inserting in the proper chronological order some titles not on our
catalogue, at the same time presenting us with copies of the works, thus
making our collection on this subject very complete.

SIOUX SPELLING BOOK, designed for the use of native
learners. By Rev. J. D. Stevens, Missionary. 12° : pp. 22.
Boston : Crocker and Brewster, for the A. B. C. F. M. 1836.

WICONI OWIHANKE WANIN TANIN KIN. 12° : pp. 23. Boston :
Crocker and Brewster, for the A. B. C. F. M. 1837.

[This little tract contains Dr. Watts' Second Catechism for Children,
translated into the Dakota Language by Joseph Renville, Sen., and Dr. T. S.
Williamson.]

THE DAKOTA FIRST READING BOOK. By Gideon H. Pond
and Stephen R. Riggs. 18° : pp. 50. Cincinnati, Ohio :
Kendall and Henry, for the A. B. C. F. M. 1839.

JOSEPH OYAKAPI KIN. The Story of Joseph and his Brethren,
translated from Genesis by Revs. Gideon H. and Samuel W.
Pond. 18° : pp. 40. Cincinnati : Kendall and Henry, for the
A. B. C. F. M. 1839.

EXTRACTS from Genesis and the Psalms : with the Third
Chapter of Proverbs, and the Third Chapter of Daniel, in the
Dakota Language. Translated from the French Bible as pub-
lished by the Am. Bible Society, by Joseph Renville, Sr.
Compared with other translations, and prepared for the press

by Thomas S. Williamson, M. D., Missionary. Cincinnati:
Kendall and Henry, for the A. B. C. F. M. 18°: pp. 72. 1839.

WOTANIN WAXTE MARKUS OWA KIN. The Gospel according
to Mark, in the Language of the Dakotas. Translated from the
French by Joseph Renville, Sr.: written out and prepared for
the press by Dr. Thomas S. Williamson, Missionary. Cincinnati: Kendall and Henry, for the A. B. C. F. M. 18°: pp.
96. 1839.

EXTRACTS from the Gospels of Matthew, Luke, and John, from
the Acts of the Apostles, and from the First Epistle of John,
in the Language of the Dakota or Sioux Indians. Translated
from the French as published by the Am. Bible Society, by
Joseph Renville, Sr. Written and prepared for the press by
Thomas S. Williamson, M. D., Missionary. Cincinnati: Kendall and Henry. 18°: pp. 48. 1839.

WOWAPI MITAWA: TAMAKOCE KAGA. My Own Book. Pre-
pared from Rev. T. H. Gallaudet's "Mother's Primer," and
" Child's Picture Defining and Reading Book," in the Dakota
Language. By S. R. Riggs, A. M., Missionary of the A. B. C.
F. M. Boston: Crocker and Brewster. Square 12°: pp. 64.
1842.

WOWAPI INONPA. The Second Dakota Reading Book. Con-
sisting of Bible Stories from the Old Testament. By Rev.
S. W. Pond. Boston: Crocker and Brewster, for the A. B. C.
F. M. 18°: pp. 54. 1842.

DAKOTA DOWANPI KIN. Dakota Hymns. Boston: Crocker
and Brewster, for the A. B. C. F. M. 18°: pp. 97. 1842.
[These Hymns were composed in the Dakota Language by Mr. Joseph
Renville and sons, and the Missionaries of the Am. Board.—S. R. R.]

WOAHOPE WIKCEMNA KIN. (Sheet.) The Ten Command-
ments and the Lord's Prayer, in the Dakota Language. Boston.
1842.

ELIZA MARPI-COKAWIN, Raratonwan Oyato en Wapiye sa:
qa Sara Warpanica qon. A narrative of pious Indian women.
Prepared in Dakota by Mrs. M. A. C. Riggs. Boston: Crocker
and Brewster, for the Am. Tract Society. 12°: pp. 12. 1842.

WICOICAGE WOWAPI QA ODOWAN WAKAN, ETC. The Book of Genesis, a part of the Psalms, and the Gospels of Luke and John. Cincinnati,Ohio: Kendall and Barnard, for the A. B. C. F. M. 12°: pp. 295. 1842.

[These translations were made partly from the original Hebrew and Greek, and partly from the French, by Dr. T. S. Williamson, Rev. G. H. Pond, S. R. Riggs, and Joseph Renville, Sen. 1—S. R. R.]

JESUS OHNIHDEWICAYE CIN ARANYANPI QON; qa Palos Wowapi kage ciqon; nakun, Jan Woyake ciqon dena cepi. Tamakoce okaga. The Acts of the Apostles, and the Epistles of Paul; with the Revelation of John; in the Dakota Language. Translated from the. Greek, by Stephen R. Riggs, A. M. Published by the Am. Bible Society. Cincinnati: Kendall and Barnard. 12°: pp. 228. 1843.

DAKOTA WIWANGAPI WOWAPI. Catechism in the Dakota or Sioux Language. By Rev. S. W. Pond, Misssionary of the A. B. C. F. M. New Haven, Conn.: Printed by Hitchcock and Stafford. 12°: pp. 12. 1844.

DAKOTA TAWOONSPE. Wowapi I. Tamakoce kaga. Dakota Lessons. Book I. By S. R. Riggs, A. M., Missionary of A. B. C. F. M. Louisville, Ky.: Morton and Griswold. Square 12°: pp. 48. 1850.[2]

DAKOTA TAWOONSPE. Wowapi II. Dakota Lessons. Book II. By S. R. Riggs, Missionary, etc. Louisville, Ky.: Morton and Griswold. Square 12°: pp. 48. 1850.[2]

DAKOTA TAWAXITKU KIN. The Dakota Friend, a small monthly paper in Dakota and English, published at Saint Paul by the Dakota Mission. Rev. G. H. Pond, Editor. 1850-2.

[In all, 20 numbers were published. The first 12 (Vol. I) were in a small three column size. The second volume was enlarged to four columns. The first number was issued in Nov. 1850. It is asserted that there is but one other instance known of a periodical being published in an American aboriginal tongue, viz., among the Cherokees.—W.]

---

1. Mr. Renville died at Lac qui Parle in 1846. Notices of him may be found in Rev. E. D. Neill's History of Minnesota, and also in "The Gospel among the Dakotas" by S. R. Riggs.

2. The printing of these two little books was superintended by Rev Robert Hopkins, who was drowned at Traverse des Sioux on the 4th of July, 1851.

GRAMMAR AND DICTIONARY of the Dakota Language, collected by the members of the Dakota Mission. By Rev. S. R. Riggs, A. M., Missionary of A. B. C. F. M. Under the patronage of the Historical Society of Minnesota. Printed by R. Craighead, 53 Vesey Street, New York, 1852; for the Smithsonian Institution, Washington City. 4°: pp. 34; 338.

AN ENGLISH AND DAKOTA VOCABULARY. By Mrs. M. A. C. Riggs. 8°: pp. 120. 1852. [This material is included in the larger work, put in this smaller form for the use of Dakota schools.]

[Having lived twenty-eight years in Minnesota, twenty-five of which was among the Dakotas, Mrs. Riggs died in Beloit, Wis., March 22, 1869.]

DAKOTA ODOWAN. Hymns in the Dakota Language with Tunes. Edited by S. R. Riggs, Missionary of A. B. C. F. M. Published by the American Tract Society, New York. 1855. 12°: pp. 127.

THE PILGRIM'S PROGRESS, by John Bunyan; in the Dakota language; translated by Stephen R. Riggs, A. M., Missionary of A. B. C. F. M.. Published by the American Tract Society, 150 Nassau Street, New York. 18°: pp. 264. 1857.

[A second edition has been printed. From this on, our books have been nearly all stereotyped.—S. R. R.]

THE CONSTITUTION OF MINNESOTA, in the Dakota language; translated by Stephen R. Riggs, A. M. By order of the Hazlewood Republic. Boston: Press of T. R. Marvin & Son, 42 Congress Street. 12°: pp. 36. 1858.

WOWAPI NITAWA. Your own Book. A Dakota Primer for schools. By S. R. Riggs. Square 12°: pp. 32. Minneapolis. 1863.

DAKOTA ODOWAN. Hymns in the Dakota Language. Edited by Stephen R. Riggs and John P. Williamson, Missionaries of the A. B. C. F. M. Published by the American Tract Society, New York. 1863. 18°: pp. 162.

[This book is electrotyped. Four editions have been printed. To the last, published in 1869, twenty pages of new matter were added. The book now has pp. 182, and contains 170 Hymns and Chants. The initials of the authors are appended—"Mr. R.," "J. R.," "A. R.," "T. S. W.," "G. H. P.," "S. W. P.," "J. P. W.," "A. W. H.," "L. L." and "A. D. F."]1

DAKOTA WIWICAWANGAPI KIN. Dakota Catechism. Prepared / from the Assembly's Shorter Catechism. By S. R. Riggs, Missionary of A. B. C. F. M. Published by the American Tract Society, New York. 24°: pp. 36. 1864.

[Two editions have been printed.]

WOONSPE ITAKIHNA. EHAKEUN OKAGA. "Precept upon Precept," translated into the Dakota Language by John B. Renville. Prepared for the press by S. R. Riggs. Published by the American Tract Society, Boston. 18°: pp. 228. 1864.

OOWA WOWAPI. The book of Letters ; an illustrated school book. By John P. Williamson, Missionary of A. B. C. F. M. Printed for the mission by the American Tract Society, New York. 12°: pp. 84. 1865.

DAKOTA WOWAPI WAKAN KIN. The New Testament in the Dakota Language ; translated from the original Greek, by Stephen R. Riggs, A. M., Missionary of the A. B. C. F. M. New York: American Bible Society. 16°: pp. 408. 1865.

WICOICAGE WOWAPI, MOWIS OWA: qa Wicoie Wakan kin, Solomon kaga. Pejihuta Wicashta Dakota iapi en kaga. The Books of Genesis and Proverbs in the Dakota Language ; translated from the original Hebrew, by Thomas S. Williamson, A. M., M. D. New York: American Bible Society. 1865. 16°: pp. 115.

DAKOTA A. B. C. BOOK. By S. R. Riggs. Chicago: Dean and Ottaway. Square 12°: pp. 40. 1866.

DAKOTA A. B. C. WOWAPI KIN. The Dakota Primer. By S. R. Riggs, Missionary of A. B. C. F. M. New York: American Tract Society. Square 12°: pp. 64. 1868.

THE BOOK OF PSALMS. Translated from the Hebrew into the

1 The initals "A. W. H." and "A. D. F." stand for Amos W. Huggins and Antoine D. Freniere. The former was killed at his home at Lac-qui-Parle on the 19th of August, 1862, the second day of the outbreak. Notices of Mr. Huggins may be found in "The Gospel among the Dakotas." Mr. Freniere, who was himself a half-breed, was killed by hostile Indians, in the summer of 1863, as he descended the Missouri River in a canoe, alone.—S. R. R.

6

Dakota language, by S. R. Riggs, Missionary of the A. B. C. F. M. New York: American Bible Society. 16°: pp. 133. 1869.

THE BOOKS OF EXODUS AND LEVITICUS. Translated from the Hebrew into the Dakota language, by T. S. Williamson, M. D., Missionary of A. B. C. F. M. New York: American Bible Society. 16°: pp. 65 and 47. 1869.

WAKANTANKA TI KI CANKU. [*Path to Heaven.*] By Rev. A. Ravoux. 2d edition. St. Paul: Pioneer Printing Company. 1863. 18°: pp. 88.

CALVARY WIWICAWANGAPI WOWAPI, &c. (Calvary Catechism in the Dakota language.) Translated for the Mission of St. John. Faribault, Minn.: Central Republican Office. 1864. 24°: pp. 50.

[By Rev. S. D. Hinman?]

IKCE WOCEKIYE WOWAPI. Qa Isantanka Makoce. Kin en Token Wohduze, qa okodakiciye Wakan en Tonakiya Woecon kin, hena de he Wowapi kin ce. Samuel Dutton Hinman, Missionary to Dakotas. St. Paul: Pioneer Printing Company. 1865. 12°: pp. 321.

[A translation of the Episcopal Book of Common Prayer.]

ODOWAN. [*Hymns.*] Philadelphia: McCalla & Stavely, Printers. 1869. 24°: pp. 26.

[By Rev. S. D. Hinman?]

BIOGRAPHICAL.

DELLA VITA E DEGLI Scritti di Costantino Beltrami da Bergamo. Scropritore delle Fonti del Missisipi, di Gabriele Rosa. Bergamo, dalla Tipografia Pagnoncelli: 1861. 12°: pp. 34.

COSTANTINO BELTRAMI DA BERGAMO. Notizie e Lettere pubblicate per cura del Municipio di Bergamo, e dedicate alla Societa' Storica di Minnesota. Bergamo, dalla Tipografia Pagnoncelli. 1865. 8°: pp. 134. [Photo. of Beltrami.]

SERVING OUR GENERATION. A Discourse Commemorative of

the Life Work of John D. Ford, M. D. Delivered in the First Baptist Church, Winona, Nov. 3, 1867. By Rev. George M. Stone. Winona: Green & Gile, Printers. 1867. 12°: pp. 18. [Photographic portrait.]

THE POETS AND POETRY OF MINNESOTA—See "Poetical and Literary."

TANNER, JOHN—See Tanner's Captivity.

TAOPI (or "Wounded Man")—See "The Indian Tribes," &c.

SKETCH OF J. N. NICOLLET—See vol. I, Hist. Soc. Coll.

SKETCH OF JOSEPH RENVILLE—See   do.   do.

SKETCH OF J. M. GOODHUE—See   do.   do.

SKETCH OF CONSTANTINE BELTRAMI—See Vol. II, Hist. Soc. Collections.

SKETCH OF CARVER—See Carver Centenary.

MILITARY.

CORRESPONDENCE on the Occasion of the Presentation by Major Gen. Sanford, United States Minister, Resident at the Court of Brussels, of a Battery of Steel Cannon, to the State of Minnesota, for the use of the First Minnesota Regiment of Volunteers. St. Paul: Press Printing Company. 1862. 8°: pp. 12.

[WAR RECORD OF MINNESOTA.] Annual Report of the Adjutant General of the State of Minnesota for the year ending Dec. 1, 1866, and of the Military Forces of the State, from 1861 to 1866. Saint Paul: Pioneer Printing Company. 1866. 8°: pp. 805.

HISTORY OF THE THIRD REGIMENT INFANTRY MINNESOTA VOLUNTEERS, with the Final Record of the Original Regiment. Compiled by C. W. Lombard. Faribault: Central Republican Office. 1869. Pp. 16.

MASONIC.

By-Laws of St. Paul Lodge No. 1, of Free and Accepted Masons; and of the Grand Lodge of Ohio. Adopted 1849. St. Paul: Printed by J. A. Aitkenside. 1849. 16°: pp. 36.
[Contains a brief History of the establishment of the Order in this State.]

Installation Address to St. Paul Lodge No. 3, by Brother A. C. Smith, P. M., delivered on the evening of Dec. 22, 1857, the 237th Anniversary of the Landing of the Pilgrims. Printed by order of the Lodge. St. Paul: Pioneer & Democrat Office. 8°: pp. 10.

Public Celebration of St. John the Baptist's Day, by Winona Lodge No. 18, A. F. & A. M. Dedication of their Hall and Address, by the M.·. W.·. A. T. C. Pierson, G.·. M.·., at Winona, June 24, 1863. St. Paul: Pioneer Printing Company. 1863. 8°: pp. 19.

Public Installation of the Officers of Hennepin Lodge No. 4, A. F. & A. M., at Minneapolis, Minn., Dec. 27, 1862, and Address by the M.·. W.·. A. T. C. Pierson, G.·. M.·. St. Paul: Pioneer Printing Company. 1863. 8°: pp. 19.

Proceedings of the Grand Lodge of Ancient Free and Accepted Masons, of Minnesota, at its Grand Annual Communications in the City of St. Paul; from February 25, A.·. L.·. 5853, to January 14, A.·. L.·. 5869. St. Paul: Pioneer Book and Job Printing Company. 1869. 8°: pp. 695.

Ceremonial for a Lodge of Sorrow. Compiled and Arranged by A. T. C. Pierson, 33, for Ancient Landmark Lodge, No. 5, at the request of H. L. Carver, W.·. M.·. St. Paul: Pioneer Printing Company. 1869. 12°: pp. 19.

RAILROADS.

The Railroad System of the State of Minnesota, with its Connections. By James W. Taylor. Reported to the Common Council of the City of St. Paul, March 31, 1859, in pursuance of a Resolution of the City Council. 1,000 copies ordered printed by the St. Paul Common Council. St. Paul: Geo. W. Moore, City Printer. 1859. 8°: pp. 22.

AN ACT PROPOSING A LOAN of State Credit to the Land Grant Railroad Companies; with arguments in favor of its Approval by the People. St. Paul: Pioneer and Democrat Office. 8°: pp. 32.

ISSUE OF MINNESOTA STATE BONDS TO LAND GRANT RAILROADS. St. Paul: Pioneer and Democrat Office. 1858. 8°: pp. 8.

IN SUPREME COURT OF THE UNITED STATES, DECEMBER TERM, 1855. The United States vs. the Minnesota and North Western Railroad Company. Motion for the United States. C. Cushing, Attorney General. 8°: pp. 11.

MEMORIAL of the Minnesota and North Western Railroad Company to His Excellency James Buchanan, President of the United States. 1857. New York: 8°: pp. 12.

CHARTER, BY-LAWS AND RULES AND REGULATIONS of the Minneapolis and Cedar Valley Railroad Company. Adopted by the Board of Directors at a Session held at Northfield, July 9, 1857. St. Paul: Goodrich, Somers &·Co., Printers. 1857.

FIRST ANNUAL REPORT of the President and Directors of the Minnesota Central Railway Company; with the Report of the Chief Engineer and Superintendent; also, a Compilation of Acts of the Legislature,.and of Congress, relating to the same. January 1, 1866. Minneapolis: 1866. 8°: pp. 88.

AN ACT TO INCORPORATE the Nininger and St. Peter Western Railroad Company. Approved March 4, 1857. St. Paul: Goodrich, Somers & Co., Printers. 1857. 8°: pp. 13.

THE MINNESOTA VALLEY RAILROAD COMPANY, ST. PAUL, MINNESOTA. Organized March 16, 1864. Grants of Land, Charter and Laws upon which the organization is based. St. Paul: Pioneer Office. 1866. 8°: pp. 46.

TRUST DEED, Securing the First Mortgage Bonds, with Plan of Preferred Stock, First and Second Issue. Minnesota Valley Railroad Company, St. Paul, June, 1867. Ramaley & Hall, Printers. 8°: pp. 39.

THE MINNESOTA VALLEY RAILROAD, forming Part of the Extension of the Union Pacific Railroad, via Sioux City and St. Paul, to Lake Superior.   Its Construction and Resources. Office, St. Paul, Minnesota.   New York: 1868.   8°: pp. 8. [Map.]

AGREEMENT AND MORTGAGE of St. Paul and Sioux City Railroad Company, Securing Special Stock.   St. Paul: Dispatch Printing Company.   8°: pp. 16.   [n. d.]

GRANT OF LANDS to the Minnesota and Pacific Railroad Company, and others, together with Act of Congress in Relation to the Same.   St. Paul: Goodrich, Somers & Co., Printers.   1857. 8°: pp. 27.

—— Do.   Do.   The Acceptance of the Grant, and By-Laws of the Company.   St. Paul: Goodrich, Somers & Co., Printers. 1857.   8°: pp. 39.

FIRST REPORT of the Officers of the Minnesota and Pacific Railroad Company.   Presented January 12, 1858.   St. Paul: Goodrich, Somers & Co., Printers.   8°: pp. 20.

FIRST DIVISION of the St. Paul and Pacific Railroad Company, St. Paul, Minn.   Organized February 6, 1864.   Grants of Land, Charter, Agreement and Proceedings upon which the Organization is based.   New York: 1865.   8°: pp. 88.   [Map.]

RAPPORT VAN DEN INGENIEUR, J. H. Kloos, omtrent den St. Paul-en Pacific Spoorweg, en de waarde der Landerijen, uitmakende het onderpand der 7 pCt Obligatien.   [Printed at Amsterdam, 1866.]   8°: pp. 14.

THE FIRST DIVISION of the St. Paul and Pacific Railroad Company, St. Paul, Minnesota.   Main Line, from St. Anthony to Breckenridge.   Organized February 6, 1864.   Grants of Land, Charter, &c.   St. Paul: 1868.   8°: pp. 84.

GUIDE TO THE LANDS of the First Division of the St. Paul and Pacific Railroad Company.   Main and Branch Lines, &c. St. Paul, Minnesota: Pioneer Printing Company.   1868.   8°: pp. 25.   [Numerous Maps.]

A GUIDE TO THE WINONA AND ST. PETER RAILROAD LANDS: Winona, Minn.   1865.   Milwaukee: Sentinel Printing House. 8°: pp. 11.

SOUTHERN MINNESOTA RAILROAD COMPANY. Prospectus, with Charter, Land Grants, Map, Statistics, etc. New York: Brown & Hewitt, Printers, 37 Park Row. 1865. 8°: pp. 78. [Map.]

—— Do. Another edition: 1868. pp. 32. [Map.]

PROSPECTUS OF THE SOUTHERN MINNESOTA RAILROAD. Maps and Statistics. * * New York: Brown & Hewitt, Printers, 30 Frankfort street. 1869. 8°: pp. 20. [Maps.]

STATEMENT OF THE St. PAUL AND CHICAGO RAILWAY COMPANY. Respecting the issue of its First Mortgage Land Grant Sinking Fund Bonds, &c. St. Paul: Ramaley & Hall, Commercial Office. 1867. 8°: pp. 15. [Map.]

CIRCULAR of the Burlington, Cedar Rapids and Minnesota Railway Company. [N. Y., 1869.] 8°: pp. 36. [Map.]

AN ACT to Incorporate the Lake Superior and Mississippi Railroad Company, approved March 8, 1861. Also, An Amendment, approved March 6, 1863. St. Paul: Press Printing Company. 1863. 8°: pp. 15.

STATE AND CONGRESSIONAL LEGISLATION relating to the Lake Superior and Mississippi Railroad Company. St. Paul: Press Print. 1864. 8°: pp. 33.

—— Do. With report of the Engineer. pp. 33.

LEGISLATION RELATING to the Lake Superior and Mississippi Railroad Company. Printed by D. Ramaley. St. Paul: 1864. 8°: pp. 24.

REPORT OF THE ENGINEER of the Lake Superior and Mississippi Railroad Co. St. Paul: Press Print. 1864. 8°: pp. 7.

THE LAKE SUPERIOR AND MISSISSIPPI RAILROAD, Connecting the Mississippi and Minnesota Rivers and the Railroad System of Minnesota and California with Lake Superior. St. Paul: Press Printing Company. 1864. 8°: pp. 11.

—— Do. Another edition, with Map. pp. 56. Press Printing Company. 1866.

—— Do. Another edition, [no imprint.] pp. 71. [Map.]

—— Do. Another edition. Press Printing Company. 1868. pp. 76. [Map.]

PACIFIC RAILROAD SURVEYS. Letter from the Secretary of War, [Jeff. Davis] transmitting Reports of Surveys, &c., of Railroad Routes to the Pacific Ocean. [House of Reps. Ex. Doc. No. 46, 33d Cong., 1st session, February 6, 1854.] 8°: pp. 118.

REPORTS OF EXPLORATIONS AND SURVEYS, to ascertain the most practicable and economical Route for a Railroad from the Mississippi River to the Pacific Ocean. Made under the direction of the Secretary of War, in 1853–4, according to Acts of Congress of March 3, 1853; May 31, 1854, and August 5, 1854. [Thirteen Volumes, quarto.] Washington: 1855–60.

SINGLE PAPERS.

1. Route near the 47th and 49th Paralells of North Latitude. Vol. 1. pp. 39–55.

2. Synopsis of a report of the Reconnoisance of a Railroad Route from Puget Sound via South Pass to the Mississippi River. By Fred. W. Lander, Civil Engineer. Washington, D. C., 1856. pp. 45. Vol. II.

Volume XII, Parts I and II, are wholly devoted to the Northern Route, vis :

Part I. 1. Narrative and final Report of Exploration for a Route for a Pacific Railroad near the 47th and 49th paralells of North Latitude, from St. Paul to Puget Sound, by Isaac I. Stevens, Governor of Washington Territory. 1855. pp. 858: 41. [2 Maps. 1 Profile, 70 Engravings.]

Part II. 2. Botanical Report. pp. 7–76; 6 plates. 3; Zoological Report; pp. 1–399. Plates 76.

THE GREAT COMMERCIAL PRIZE, addressed to every American who values the prosperity of his country. By Charles C. Coffin, a member of the Boston Press. Boston: A. Williams & Co., 100 Washington street. 1858. 8°: pp. 23.

SPEECH OF HON. JAMES SHIELDS, of Minnesota, on the Pacific Railroad Bill; delivered in the Senate of the United States, January 7, 1859. Washington: 1859. 8°: pp. 6.

PACIFIC RAILROAD. Minority Report, of Hon. C. Aldrich, from the Select Committee on the Pacific Railroad, submitting considerations in favor of the Northern Route. House Doc. No. 428, 36th Cong., 1st Sess., April 16, 1860. 8°: pp. 9.

PACIFIC RAILROAD—NORTHERN ROUTE. Letter of Hon. Isaac I. Stevens, Delegate from Washington Territory, to the Railroad Convention of Washington and Oregon, called to meet at Vancouver, W. T., May 20, 1860. Washington: T. McGill, Printer. 1860. 8°: pp. 24.

NORTHERN PACIFIC RAILROAD COMPANY. Policy for the management of its affairs, adopted by the Board of Directors, Jan. 11, 1865. 8°: pp. 4. [No imprint.]

BOSTON BOARD OF TRADE. Report on the Northern Pacific Railroad, made to the Government of the Board, and unanimously adopted, November 27, 1865. Boston: 1865. 8°: pp. 22.

NORTHERN PACIFIC RAILROAD. Memorial of the Board of Direction of the Company, with communications from Lieut. Gen. Grant, Br. Maj. Gen. Meigs, Q. M. G.; and Brv. Maj. Gen. Ingalls, A. Q. M.; and Report of the Engineer in Chief. Nov., 1867. [Senate Mis. Doc. No. 9, 40th Cong., 2d Sess., Dec. 17, 1867.] 8°: pp. 39. [Map.]

—— Same; another edition. Case, Lockwood & Co., Hartford: pp. 56. [2 Maps.]

NORTHERN PACIFIC RAILROAD. Statement of its Resources and Merits, as presented to the Pacific Railroad Committee of Congress, H. R., by Hon. J. Gregory Smith, Hon. R. D. Rice, of Maine; Hon. Wm. B. Ogden, of Chicago; Gov. Marshall, of Minn., and Edwin F. Johnson, Civ. Eng., March, 1868. Washington: Intelligencer Pr. House. 8°: pp. 24.

LETTER upon the Agricultural and Mineral Resources of the North-Western Territories, on the Route of the Northern Pacific Railroad. By Philip Ritz, of Walla Walla. Chronicle Print, Washington, D. C. [1868.] 8°: pp. 8.

THE NORTHERN PACIFIC RAILWAY; its effect upon the Public Credit, the Public Revenues, and the Public Debt. Speech of Hon. William Windom, of Minnesota, delivered in the House of Representatives, January 5, 1869. Washington: Gibson Brothers, Printers. 1869. 8°: pp. 60.

THE POLICY OF EXTENDING GOVERNMENT AID to additional Railroads to the Pacific, by Guaranteeing interest on their Bonds. Report of the Majority of the Senate Committee on Pacific Railroad. February 19, 1869. [Senate Doc. No. 219, 40th Cong., 3d Session.] 8°: pp. 31.

7

NORTHERN PACIFIC RAILROAD. Report of Edwin F. Johnson, Engineer in Chief, to the Board of Directors. April, 1869. Hartford: 1869.   8°: pp. 78.   [6 maps.]

SOCIETIES AND CONVENTIONS.

INDEPENDENT ORDER OF ODD FELLOWS. Proceedings of the R. W. Grand Lodge of Minnesota. 1854 to 1869.   8°: pp. 528.

JOURNAL of the Second Sitting of the Third House of Sovereigns. Saturday Evening, Feb. 16, 1856.   Sol. Smith, Printer to the "Sovereigns."   8°: pp. 15.

—— Do. Third Session. Printed at the expense of the Sovereigns: 1860.   8°: pp. 24.

REPORTS of the Agricultural and Mechanical Club of the Minnesota Legislature, held at the State House, St. Paul, during the Winter of 1859–60.   Minneapolis: Hyde & Williams, Minnesota Beacon Office.   8°: pp. 32.

THIRD ANNUAL FAIR of the Hennepin County Agricultural Society, to be held at Minneapolis, Sept. 26, 27 and 28, 1865. Atlas Printing Company, Minneapolis, Minn.: 1865.   8°: pp. 15.

FOURTH ANNUAL FAIR, do.   1866.   Pp. 21.

PREMIUM LIST and Rules and Regulations of the 8th Annual Fair of the Minnesota State Agricultural Society, to be held at the Fair Ground in Rochester, on the 2d, 3d, 4th and 5th of October, 1866.   Atlas Printing Company, Minneapolis: 1866. 8°: pp. 35.

—— Do. 10th Annual Fair, at Minneapolis, 1868.   Pp. 31.

—— Do. 11th "   " at Rochester, 1869.   Pp. 31.

PROCEEDINGS OF THE FIRST ANNUAL MEETING of the Minnesota Editors' and Publishers' Association, held at St. Paul, February 20 and 21, 1867.   12°: pp. 21.

—— Do. For 1868.   8°: pp. 22.

—— Do. For 1869.   8°: pp. 36.

PROCEEDINGS OF THE CONVENTION OF COLORED CITIZENS of the State of Minnesota, in Celebration of the Anniversary of Emancipation, and the Reception of the Electoral Franchise, on the First of January, 1869. St. Paul: Press Print. 1869. 8°: pp. 31.

TRANSACTIONS OF THE MINNESOTA STATE MEDICAL SOCIETY. St. Paul: Pioneer Book and Job Printing Company. 1870. 8°: pp. 46.

SCHOOL AND COLLEGE CATALOGUES.

CATALOGUES OF THE BALDWIN SCHOOL and the Academic Department of the College of St. Paul, Minnesota. MDCCCLIV. St. Paul: Printed at the Minnesotian Office. 1854. 8°: pp. 15.

ADDRESSES AT DEDICATION OF BALDWIN SCHOOL: see " Saint Paul."

CIRCULAR AND CATALOGUE of the Saint Paul Female Seminary, Saint Paul, Minnesota. 1858–1861. St. Paul: Pioneer Print. 1861. 8°: pp. 12.

—— Do. For 1862–1864. Printed by F. Somers, New York. Pp. 16.

FIRST ANNUAL CATALOGUE of the Preparatory Department of the Hamline University, Red Wing, Minn., Aug., 1855. Red Wing: Meritt & Hutchins, Printers. 1855. 8°: pp. 17.

BIENNIAL CATALOGUE of Hamline University, for the Collegiate Year 1859–60. Red Wing, Minnesota: Hubbard & Davis, Printers. 1860. 8°: pp. 20.

—— Catalogue for year ending June, 1863. 8°: pp. 24.

—— Do. For year ending June, 1866. 8°: pp. 31.

" HAMLINE UNIVERSITY MAGAZINE :" see " Magazines."

CATALOGUE OF THE OFFICERS AND STUDENTS of the Minnesota Seminary, Wasioja, Dodge Co. Wasioja: " Minnesota Free Will Baptist" Office. 1861. 8°: pp. 24.

FIRST ANNUAL CIRCULAR AND CATALOGUE of the Sigourney Boarding School, St. Anthony, Minnesota. 1860–61. St. Anthony : Thomas & Clarke, Printers. 1861.

FIRST ANNUAL REGISTER of the Minnesota State Normal School, at Winona, for the Academical year 1866–67. Winona, September, 1867 : Republican Print. 8° : pp. 22.

UNIVERSITY OF MINNESOTA. Catalogue of the Officers and Students of the Preparatory Department, with a Statement of the Courses of Instruction, 1867–8, St. Anthony, Aug., 1868. Published by the University. Minneapolis : Tribune Print. 8° : pp. 20.

REPORT OF THE COMMITTEE ON ORGANIZATION, made to the Board of Regents of the University of Minnesota, May 7, 1869. Published by the Board. Minneapolis : Tribune Printing Co. 1869. 8° : pp. 38.

ANNUAL CATALOGUES AND CIRCULARS of the Shattuck Grammar School, Faribault, Minn. Faribault : Central Republican Office. 12°. 1866–1869.

CATALOGUE OF THE INSTRUCTORS AND MEMBERS of the State Teachers' Institute, Minnesota. [From March 29, to May 11, 1868.] Republican Printing House, Winona. 1868. 8° : pp. 21.

—— Do. 1868. 8° : pp. 34.

THE FIRST ANNUAL CATALOGUE of Northfield College, Northfield, Minn., July, 1868. H. A. Kimball, Printer. 8° : pp. 12.

CATALOGUE OF THE SCHOOLS of the Bishop Seabury Mission, 1865–6, Faribault, Minn. Central Republican Office. 1866. 8° : pp. 28.

DIOCESE OF MINNESOTA. Saint Mary's Hall Register, Faribault. Faribault : Central Republican Office. 12°. 1867 to 1869. v. d.

CHURCHES AND RELIGIOUS ASSOCIATIONS.

MINUTES of the Minnesota Baptist Association. 1852–1869. 12°. *v. d.*

—— Do. Minnesota Central Baptist Association. 1858–1869. 12°. *v. d.*

—— Do. Anniversaries of the Minnesota Baptist State Convention. 1859–1869. 8°. *v. d.*

—— Do. Northern Baptist Association. 1861–1869. 8°. *v. d.*

—— Do. Zumbro Baptist Association. 1861–1869. 8°. *v. d.*

—— Do. Minnesota Valley Baptist Association. 1859–1869. 12°. *v. d.*

—— Do. Southern Minnesota Baptist Association. 1855–1869. 8°. *v. d.*

——Do. Crow River Baptist Association. 1868–1869. 12°. *v. d.*

MINUTES of the Minnesota Annual Conference of the Methodist Episcopal Church. 1856–1869. 8°. *v. d.*

MINUTES of the Annual Sessions of the General Conference of the Congregational Churches in Minnesota. 1856–1869. 8°. *v. d.*

JOURNAL of the Proceedings of the Annual Conventions of the Protestant Episcopal Church in the Diocese of Minnesota. 1856–1869. 8°. *v. d.*

RECORD of the Organization and First Session of the Synod of Minnesota, with the Opening Discourse, by the Rev. Thos. S. Williamson, M. D. St. Paul: Daily Minnesotian Print. 1858. 8°: pp. 14.

A HAND BOOK for the Presbyterian Church in Minnesota, designed to promote order in, and love for the Sanctuary. Prepared by Edward D. Neill. Philadelphia: Printed by Henry B. Ashmead. 1856. 24°: pp. 72.

MANUAL of the First Presbyterian Church of Red Wing, Minn., with a Brief Historical Sketch. Red Wing: Republican Office. 1868. 24°: pp. 38.

PARISH MANUAL of the Church of Gethsemane, Minneapolis, Minn.; Organized A. D. 1856., Minneapolis: 1869. pp. 18.

A MEMORIAL to the Board of Trustees of the Minnesota Church Foundation, with additions and an appendix. Containing the Charter and By-Laws of the Board, and the Charter of "Christ Church Orphans' Home and Hospital for Minnesota." By the Rev. J. V. Van Ingen, D. D. St. Paul: Pioneer Printing Co. 1860. 8°: pp. 34.

MISSION PAPER of the Bishop Seabury Mission. Numbers 1 to 37. 8°. Faribault. *v. d.*

ELEVENTH ANNIVERSARY of the Minnesota Bible Society, held in the First Presbyterian Church, St. Paul, June 8, 1862, 7½ P. M. St. Paul: Press Printing Co. 1862. 8°: pp. 7.

FOURTEENTH do.; with its Constitution, List of Officers, and Local Agents of Auxiliaries. St. Paul, Minn., June, 1864. David Ramaley, Printer. 8°: pp. 32.

ANNUAL REPORT OF THE STATE CENTRAL COMMITTEE to the Minnesota Sabbath-School Association, assembled in Convention at Hastings, June 26, 1866. 8°: pp. 14.

—— Do. Rochester, June 18, 1867. Pp. 15.

PROCEEDINGS of the Tenth Annual Convention of the Minnesota State Sabbath-School Association, held at Faribault, June 16, 17, and 18, 1868. Published for the Association. 1868. 8°: pp. 72.

PROCEEDINGS of the Minnesota Universalist Sunday-School State Convention, including the articles of Incorporation and Constitution of the Convention, &c. First Annual Session. Held at Minneapolis, Sept. 1st and 2d, 1869. St. Paul: 1869. 8°: pp. 18.

FIRST ANNUAL REPORT AND CONSTITUTION of the Brotherhood of the Parish of the Good Shepherd, Faribault, Minn. Published by the Brotherhood. Central Republican Office. 1870. 12°: pp. 16.

THE PAPAL ENCYCLICAL. A Pastoral Letter: see "Sermons," &c.

HISTORICAL SKETCH OF WESTMINSTER PRESB. CHURCH: see "Sermons," &c.

MANUAL OF FIRST BAPTIST CHURCH, ST. PAUL: see "St. Paul."

GOSPEL AMONG THE DAKOTAS: see "Indian Tribes of Minnesota."

SERMONS AND RELIGIOUS ESSAYS.

THE POLITICAL CHARACTER AND TENDENCIES OF ROMANISM: being the substance of a Discourse delivered in Galena in 1852, by Rev. M. Sorin, Red Wing, Minn. Ter. 1854.

THE TRUE THANKSGIVING ; AND TRUE MANHOOD: Two Sermons, by H. M. Nichols, Pastor of the First Presbyterian Church, Stillwater, Minn. Van Vorhes & Easton, Printers. 1858. 12°: pp. 40.

[Rev. Mr. Nichols was drowned July, 1860, at Lake Harriet, near Minneapolis.]

MICHAL ; OR FASHIONABLE DANCING, an Undignified Amusement for a Christian. The sixth of a Series of Evening Lectures on the Life of David, at the Chapel of the House of Hope, St. Paul, Minn., Feb. 6, 1859, by Edward D. Neill. St. Paul: 1859. 12°: pp. 18.

CHILDREN, AND THE CHILDHOOD OF JESUS. Sermon occasioned by the Death of Willie Young: Preached in the Jackson Street Methodist Church, on Sabbath afternoon, Feb. 27, 1859, by Rev. J. D. Pope, Pastor of the First Baptist Church. Published by the Family for Private Distribution. St. Paul: Minnesotian Office. 1859. 8°: pp. 12.

CONGREGATIONALISM. A Sunday Morning Discourse, in the Plymouth Church of St. Paul, March 20, 1859. By Burdett Hart. St. Paul: T. M. Newson, Printer. 1859: 8°: pp. 18.

BLOOD, THE PRICE OF REDEMPTION. A Thanksgiving Discourse, delivered in the House of Hope, Nov. 27, 1862, by Rev. Frederic A. Noble, Pastor. St. Paul: Press Printing Co. 1862. 8°: pp. 21.

THE FALL OF SUMPTER: ITS INTENT AND PORTENT. An Address given at Plymouth Church, St. Paul, Sunday evening, April 12, 1863, the Anniversary of the Attack on Fort Sumpter. By Rev. S. Hawley. St. Paul: Press Printing Co. 1863. 8°: pp. 18.

THE FINAL SALVATION OF ALL MANKIND, clearly demonstrated by the united Voice of Reason and Revelation. By Rev. Dolphus Skinner, D. D. Fourth Edition. Minneapolis: Atlas Pr. Co. 1864. 8°: pp. 31.

THE ASSURED AND GLORIOUS FUTURE OF THE NATION. A Thanksgiving Discourse, delivered in the House of Hope, Nov. 24, 1864, by Rev. Frederic A. Noble. St. Paul, Minnesota. "Ye shall be as the Wings of a Dove Covered with Silver." St. Paul: David Ramaley, Printer. 1864. 8°: pp. 28.

A SERMON Preached at the Dedication of the First Presbyterian Church, Mankato, Minn., Sept. 7, 1865, by the. Pastor, Rev. Thomas Marshall. New York: Anson D. F. Randolph. 1866. 8°: pp. 23.

THE PAPAL ENCYCLICAL, by the Rev. Thomas L. Grace, Bishop of St. Paul. Being a Pastoral Letter to the Clergy and Laity of the Diocese, on occasion of the Publication of the Jubilee. St. Paul: Pioneer Printing Company. 1865. 8°: pp. 29.

METHODISM: Its Development and the Chief Causes of its success. A Centenary Sermon, preached Sept. 21, 1866, before the Minnesota Annual Conference of the Methodist Episcopal Church. By Rev. Jabez Brooks, A. M., President of Hamline University. Published by request of the Conference. St. Paul: Press Printing Co. 1866. 8°: pp. 24.

CHRISTIAN AMUSEMENTS. A Discourse delivered Feb. 11, 1866, at the Annual Meeting of the Young Men's Christian Association of Saint Paul, by Rev. Edwin Sidney Williams. St. Paul: Davidson & Hall, Pioneer Office. 1866. 8°: pp. 31.

ADDRESS TO THE TENTH ANNUAL CONVENTION of the Diocese

of Minnesota, by Rt. Rev. Henry Benj. Whipple, D. D., Bishop of the Diocese. June 12, A. D. 1867. St. Paul: Ramaley & Hall. 1867. 8°: pp. 20.

CHRIST, NOT SELF, THE BURDEN OF CHRISTIAN PREACHING AND LIVING. A Sermon preached in St. John's Church, St. Cloud, Minn., Sept. 8, 1867, by Rev. George L. Chase, on resigning the Rectorship of the Parish. Published by request. St. Cloud, Minn.: Printed by A. J. Reed. 1867. 8°: pp. 14.

A REVIEW OF A SERMON ON THE IMMORTALITY OF THE SOUL, preached by W. B. Dada, before the Young Men's Christian Association in Lake City, April 18, 1869, by A. G. Hudson. Lake City: Leader Office. 1869. 8°: pp. 18.

UNIVERSALISM UNMASKED. A Sermon delivered by Rev. J. B. Tuttle, pastor of the Baptist Church of Anoka, Minnesota, on the evening of Feb. 14, 1869. Press Print. 8°: pp. 14.

HISTORICAL SKETCH of the Westminster Presbyterian Church of Minneapolis, Minn., [a Sermon,] by Rev. Robert F. Sample, Pastor. Philadelphia: Printed by Alfred Martin. 1869. 8°: pp. 40.

NATURAL RELIGION. By Rev. Herman Bisbee. A Sermon delivered at Pence Opera House, Minneapolis, Minn., March 27, 1870. 8°: pp. 8. [No imprint.]

HARMONY OF GOSPEL HISTORY. See "Poetical and Literary."

SERVING OUR GENERATION. A Sermon, &c. See "Biographical."

ANNIVERSARY SERMON of First Baptist Church, St. Paul. See "Saint Paul."

HAND BOOK OF PRESBYTERIAN CHURCH. See "Churches," &c.

MISSION PAPERS of Bp. Seabury Mission. See "Churches," &c.

SYNOD OF MINNESOTA. Discourse by Rev. T. S. Williamson. See "Churches," &c.

8

ORATIONS AND. ADDRESSES.

ADDRESS delivered by Ex-Governor Alexander Ramsey, Pres
ident of the Minnesota Territorial Agricultural Society, on the
occasion of the Second Annual Territorial Fair, held at Minneapolis, on the 8th, 9th and 10th of October, 1856. St. Paul:
Minnesotian Office. 1857. 8°: pp. 22.

EDUCATION IN ITS RELATIONS TO CIVILIZATION. An Address
delivered before the Convention of Superintendents at Winona,
Minn., on June 28, 1865. By Wm. F. Phelps, A. M., Principal of the State Normal School. 1865. Republican Print,
Winona. 8°: pp. 34.

THE PROBLEM OF AMERICAN DESTINY. An Oration. Deliver-
ed at a Celebration of the Grand Army of the Republic of the
State of Minnesota, at Owátonna, July 4th, 1868. By Capt.
Henry A. Castle, of St. Paul. Published by order of the G.
A. R., Dept. of Minn. St. Paul: Office of the Press Printing
Company. 1868. 8°: pp. 12.

ORATION delivered at Alexandria, Douglas Co., Minn., July
4, 1868, by Hon. H. L. Gordon, of St. Cloud. Ramaley &
Hall. Dispatch Office. 8°: pp. 16.

ADDRESSES at the Inauguration of Wm. W. Folwell, as President of the University of Minnesota, Wednesday, December
22, 1869. For the University. Minneapolis: Tribune Printing Company. 1870. 8°: pp. 40.

EMIGRANT ROUTE TO CALIFORNIA, by Col. Wm. H. Nobles.
See "Relations of Minnesota to the Northwest."

SPEECH OF HON. JAMES SHIELDS on the Pacific R. R. bill.
See "Railroads."

THE NORTHERN PACIFIC RAILWAY. Speech of Hon. Wm.
Windom. See "Railroads."

EARLY HISTORY OF HENNEPIN COUNTY, by John H. Stevens.
See "Town and County History."

ADDRESSES at Dedication of Baldwin School. See "St. Paul."

MASONIC INSTALLATION AND DEDICATION ADDRESSES. See
"Masonic."

ADDRESSES BEFORE THE HISTORICAL SOCIETY. By E. D. Neill, Gen. J. H. Simpson. Hon. Alex. Ramsey, Rev. S. R. Riggs, Gen. H. H. Sibley, Hon. J. W. Lynd, Rev. J. Mattocks, and others. See Hist. Soc. Coll., Vols. I and II.

POETICAL AND LITERARY.

THE SONNETS OF SHAKSPEARE: An Essay, by Ignatius Donnelly, A. M. Printed for private distribution. Saint Paul: Geo. W. Moore, Minnesotian Office. 8°: pp. 16. [1858.]

THE POETS AND POETRY OF MINNESOTA. Edited by Mrs. W. J. Arnold. Chicago: S. P. Rounds, Printer. 1864. 12°: pp. 336. [*Portrait.*]

THE DALYS OF DALYSTOWN. By Dillon O'Brien. St. Paul: Pioneer Printing Company. 1866. 8°: pp. 518.

MANOMIN: A Rhythmical Romance of Minnesota, the Great Rebellion and the Minnesota Massacres. By Myron Coloney. St. Louis: Published by the Author. 1866. 12°: pp. xv, 297.

HARMONY OF THE GOSPEL HISTORY, from Passion Week to Pentecost. By the Rev. Edward P. Gray. New York: H. B. Durand, 49 White Street. 1866. 8°: pp. 12.

GEDICHTE VERMISCHTEN INHALTS, von Albert Wolff. St. Paul, Minn. 1867. 24°: pp. 80.
[Poems written in the German language.]

OSSEO, THE SPECTRE CHIEFTAIN.[1] A Poem. By Evender C. Kennedy. Leavenworth: Published by the Author. 1867. 12°: pp. 228.

---

1 [The scene of this Epic is laid on Lake Pepin. The author says in his preface: "I offer this, my first endeavor as an author, to the public, hoping it may be received with favor; and will be content if I receive from my friends a kind thought in return for the many weary days and dreary nights I have spent trying to consummate this, my bloodless ambition. If I can be permitted to occupy the most secluded niche in the Temple of Calliope, and add but a single jewel to the casket of American Poetry, I will have gained the highest wish of my most ideal dreams. I entreat the favor of my many friends and fellow soldiers. I have a hope; must it be a hope of despair? I wait the revelations of the mysterious future."]

NEW AMERICAN EPIC POEM on the Discovery of America by Christopher Columbus. By M. D. C. Luby.   Saint Paul, Minn.: Daily Minnesota Volksblatt Print. 1868. 16°: pp. 253.

" EQUAL RIGHTS." A Poetical Lecture. By Mrs. F. A. Logan, of New York. Price 20 cents. [St. Paul: Press Print. 1869.] 12°: pp. 22.

MINNESOTA; Then and Now. By Mrs. Harriet E. Bishop. Saint Paul: D. D. Merrill, Randall & Co. 1869. [In verse.] 12°: pp. 100.

THE ROMANCE OF INDIAN LIFE.   See "The Indian Tribes of Minnesota."

A SUMMER IN THE WILDERNESS, &c. See "Early Explorations," &c.

THE HAMLINE UNIVERSITY MAGAZINE.   See " Magazines."

MAGAZINES.

THE MINNESOTA FARMER AND GARDENER. Edited by L. M. Ford and J. H. Stevens. St. Paul: Vol. I. Nov. 1860 to Dec. 1861. 8°: pp. 384.

THE HAMLINE UNIVERSITY MAGAZINE. " Religio, Litera, Libertas." Vol. 1, Nos. 1, 2, 3. 8°: pp. 24, 32, 32. Printed for the University by D. Ramaley. 1864-65.

THE MINNESOTA TEACHER AND JOURNAL OF EDUCATION: Organ of the Department of Public Instruction and State Teachers' Association. W. W. Payne, Editor and publisher, St. Paul. 8°. Vol. I, June, 1867, to Aug., 1868, 556 pages; Vol. II, Sept., 1868, to Sept., 1869, 448 pages.

THE MINNESOTA MONTHLY: A North Western Magazine. The Official Organ of the Patrons of Husbandry. Devoted to Agriculture, Horticulture, Domestic Economy, etc. Edited by D. A. Robertson. Vol. I, Jan. to Dec., 1869. Pp. 444.

SAINT PAUL.

ORDINANCES OF THE TOWN OF SAINT PAUL, MINNESOTA. In force Jan. 25, 1852. Collated and Printed by Order of the President and Council of said Town. Saint Paul : D. A. Robertson, Printer. 1852. 8° : pp. 24.

ADDRESSES delivered at the Dedication of the Edifice of the Preparatory Department of the Baldwin School,. Saint Paul, Minnesota Territory ; and Catalogue for 1853. Saint Paul : Owens & Moore, Printers. 1854. 8° : pp. 39.

CHARTER AND ORDINANCES OF THE CITY OF ST. PAUL. Minnesotian Office. 1855. 8° : pp. 111.

—— Do. 1858. Minnesotian Office. 8° : pp. 250.

—— Do. 1863. Pioneer Office. 8° : pp. 226.

—— Do. 1869. Pioneer Office. 8° : pp. 352.

PROCEEDINGS OF THE COMMON COUNCIL of the City of St. Paul for the years ending 1856 to 1870. 8°. v. d.

—— Do. General Index to. From 1854 to Jan. 19, 1858. Prepared by I. V. D. Heard, under Resolution of the Common Council, &c. Saint Paul : Pioneer Printing Co. 1866. 8° : pp. 349.

ANNUAL REPORT of the Public School System of the City of St. Paul ; with Rules and Regulations of the Board of Education, &c., &c. Saint Paul : 1856 to 1870. 12°. v. d.

SUGGESTIONS relative to the Sewerage and Street Grades of Saint Paul. [By James Starkey.] Saint Paul : Goodrich, Somers & Co., Printers and Publishers, Pioneer and Democrat Office. 1857. 12° : pp. 24.

FINANCES OF RAMSEY COUNTY. Report of a Committee of Investigation. 500 copies ordered printed by the Board of Supervisors. 1858.

GRAND CELEBRATION in the City of Saint Paul, the Capital of the State of Minnesota, on the first of September, 1858, commemorative of the successful laying and working of the Atlantic Telegraph Cable. Full Report of the Ceremonies, Processions, Illumination and the Speeches of Ex-Governors Ramsey and Gorman. Published by order of the City Council, as reported for the Daily Minnesotian, the official paper of the City, [*by J. F. Williams.*] St. Paul: Daily Minnesotian Print. 1858. 8°: pp. 22.

MANUAL of the First Baptist Church of Saint Paul, Minnesota, 1857–8; with the Annual Sermon of the Pastor [*Rev. Jno. D. Pope.*] Published by the Members. Saint Paul: Printed by Geo. W. Moore, Minnesotian Office. 1859. 8°: pp. 16.

FIRST ANNUAL REPORT of the Treasurer of the Saint Paul Gas Light Company, to the Stockholders of the Company, together with the Act of Incorporation and By-Laws. St. Paul: Pioneer Printing Company. 1859. 8°: pp. 31.

CONSTITUTION AND BY-LAWS, and Reading Room Regulations of the Saint Paul Mercantile Library Association. Adopted September, 1857. Revised Jan., 1859. Incorporated Jan., 1859. Saint Paul: Printed by Geo. W. Moore, Minnesotian Office. 1859. 8°: pp. 15.

CATALOGUE of the Sunday-School Library of the Central Presbyterian Church, Saint Paul. St. Paul: Pioneer Printing Co. 1858. 12°: pp. 20.

CATALOGUE of the St. Paul Library Association. 1864. St. Paul: Printed by D. Ramaley. 8°: pp. 79.

—— Do. 1868. Ramaley & Hall. 8°: pp. 99.

SAINT PAUL STREET RAILWAY COMPANY. Charter and City Ordinance. Saint Paul: Daily Minnesota Volksblatt Print. 1868. 8°: pp. 9.

THE EARLY HISTORY OF SAINT PAUL. Being a short sketch prepared for Bailey's Saint Paul Directory. Edition of 1867. [*Separately printed.*] By J. Fletcher Williams, Secretary of the Minnesota Historical Society, St. Paul, Minn. 1867. 8°: pp. 12. [2 cuts.]

CHAMBER OF COMMERCE OF THE CITY OF SAINT PAUL. Articles of Incorporation, By-Laws, Officers, Committees and Members. Organized Jan. 10, 1867. St. Paul, Minnesota: Press Printing Company. 1867. 8°: pp. 18.

—— Do. First Annual Report, [*By J. D. Ludden,*] for 1867. St. Paul: Press Printing Company. 1868. 8°: pp. 35.

—— Do. Second Annual Report, [*By J. D. Ludden,*] made Jan. 25, 1869. Also, Articles of Incorporation, By-Laws, Officers, and List of Members. Saint Paul: Press Printing Co. 1869. 8°: pp. 32.

—— Do. Third Annual Report. By Ossian E. Dodge, Secretary. St. Paul: Press Printing Co. 1870. 8°: pp. 51.

BUSINESS DIRECTORY for the City of Saint Paul, Minnesota Territory. Aug. 1, 1856. Saint Paul: Goodrich & Somers, Printers, Pioneer and Democrat Office. 1856. 8°: pp. 76.

SAINT PAUL CITY DIRECTORY, FOR 1856-7. Published by Goodrich & Somers ; January, 1857. Saint Paul: Pioneer and Democrat Office. 1857. 12°: pp. 194. [*Map of City. This book was compiled by Andrew Keiller.*]

COMMERCIAL ADVERTISER DIRECTORY for the City of St. Paul, to which is added, a Business Directory, 1858-1859. Newson & Barton, Publishers. Saint Paul: Times Office. 1858. 8°: pp. 165.

A. BAILEY'S SAINT PAUL DIRECTORY, FOR 1863. Volume One. Saint Paul: A. Bailey, Publisher. 1863. 8°: pp. 170.

SAINT PAUL DIRECTORY FOR 1864. Including a complete Directory of the Citizens, a Business Directory, etc. Volume Two. Saint Paul: Groff & Bailey, Publishers. 1864. 8°: pp. 170.

McCLUNG'S SAINT PAUL DIRECTORY, and Statistical Record, for 1866. Containing an Alphabetical List of Citizens in each Ward separately, etc. St. Paul: J. W. McClung, Publisher. 1866. 8°: pp. 284.

SAINT PAUL DIRECTORY FOR 1867. * * * Vol. 3. Saint Paul: Bailey & Wolfe, Publishers. 1867. 8°: pp. 287.

KETCHUM AND CRAWFORD'S ST. PAUL DIRECTORY, FOR 1869.

* * * Also, a complete Classified Business Directory, &c. St. Paul : Printed by the Press Printing Co. [1869.] 8° : pp. 271. [Map.]

RICE & BELL'S FIRST ANNUAL DIRECTORY to the Inhabitants, Institutions, &c., &c., in the City of Saint Paul, for 1869-70. Rice & Bell, Publishers, St. Paul. [1869.] 8° : pp. 300. [Map.]

HAND BOOK OF PRESBYTERIAN CHURCH. See " Churches," &c.

. CHRIST'S CHURCH ORPHAN'S HOME. See " Churches," &c.

INSTALLATION ADDRESS TO ST. PAUL LODGE, No. 3. See " Masonic."

BALDWIN SCHOOL, and Female Seminary Catalogues. See " Catalogues."

CARVER CENTENARY. See Histor. Soc. Coll.

MEMORIAL OF CHAMBER OF COMMERCE, &c. See " Relations of Minnesota to the North West."

RISE AND PROGRESS OF MINNESOTA TERRITORY. See " Historical, Descriptive," &c.

DAKOTA LAND ; or the Beauty of St. Paul. See " Historical, Descriptive," &c.

STATE DOCUMENTS.

JOURNAL OF THE COUNCIL of the Legislative Assembly of the Territory of Minnesota. 1849-1857. 8°. *v. d.*

JOURNAL OF THE HOUSE OF REPRESENTATIVES of the Legislative Assembly of the Territory of Minnesota. 1849-1857. 8°. *v. d.*

ACTS, JOINT RESOLUTIONS AND MEMORIALS passed by the Legislative Assembly of the Territory of Minnesota. 1849-18 57. 8°. *v. d.*

DEBATES AND PROCEEDINGS of the Constitutional Convention for the Territory of Minnesota. to form a State Constitution, etc. T. F. Andrews, Official Reporter to the Convention. St. Paul: G. W. Moore, Printer. 1858. 8°: pp. 624. [*Republican Wing.*]

THE DEBATES AND PROCEEDINGS of the Minnesota Constitutional Convention, including the Organic Act of the Territory, etc.' Reported Officially by Francis H. Smith. Saint Paul: E. S. Goodrich, Territorial Printer. 1857. 8°: pp. 685. [*Democratic Wing.*]

JOURNAL OF THE CONSTITUTIONAL CONVENTION of the Territory of Minnesota, [*Democratic Wing,*] begun and held in the City of St. Paul, Capital of said Territory, on Monday, the 13th of July, 1857. St. Paul: Earle S. Goodrich, State Printer. 1857. 8°: pp. 208.

JOURNAL OF THE SENATE of the Legislature of the State of Minnesota. 1858-1870. 8°. *v. d.*

JOURNAL OF THE HOUSE OF REPRESENTATIVES of the State of Minnesota. 1858-1870. 8°. *v. d.*

GENERAL AND SPECIAL LAWS of the State of Minnesota. 1858-1870. 8°. *v. d.*

EXECUTIVE DOCUMENTS of the State of Minnesota. 1860-1870. 8°. *v. d.*

THE LEGISLATIVE MANUAL, compiled for the use of the Members of the Legislature. Published by authority. 1860-1870. *v. d.*

ANNUAL REPORT of the Adjutant General of the State of Minnesota, for the year ending Dec. 1, 1866, and of the Military forces of the State from 1861 to 1866. Saint Paul: Pioneer Printing Company. 1866. 8°: pp. 805.

A COMPLETE COMPILATION OF THE LAWS OF MINNESOTA, relating to Township Organization, and the duties of Town Officers, etc. By Elijah M. Haines. Chicago: 1869. 8°: pp. 272.

REPORTS OF CASES ARGUED AND DETERMINED in the Supreme Court of Minnesota. 13 vols. 8°. St. Paul. 1858-1870. *v. d.*

— Harvey Officer, Reporter. Vols. I-IX.

— Wm. A. Spencer, Reporter. Vols. X-XIII.

9

THE REVISED STATUTES OF THE TERRITORY OF MINNESOTA, passed at the 2d session of the Legislative Assembly, commencing Jan. 1, 1851. Under the Supervision of M. S. Wilkinson. Saint Paul: James M. Goodhue, Territorial Printer. Rl. 8°: pp. 734.

—— Do. Edition of 1859. Rl. 8°: pp. 1071. Pioneer Printing Co., St. Paul. 1859.

—— Do. Revision of 1866. Rl. 8°: pp. 874. Davidson & Hall. 1867.

MAGAZINE ARTICLES.

HARPERS' NEW MONTHLY MAGAZINE. Vols. 1 to 38. New York.

PAPERS ON MINNESOTA.

Vol. VII, p. 177. Sketches of the Upper Mississippi. Anon.
" XIII, p. 665. A Visit to Red River. Anon.
" XVI, p. 443. The Upper Mississippi. Anon.
" XVIII, p. 169. The People of the Red River. Anon.
" do. p. 602. The Red River Trail. Anon.
" XIX, p. 37. The Red River Trail. Anon.
" XXI, p. 289. To Red River and Beyond. By Manton Marble.
" do. p. 581. "   ",   "   "   "
" XXII, p. 306. "   "   "   "   "
" XXVI, p. 186. Hole-in-the-Day. By I. G. Nicolay.
" XXVII, p. 1. The Indian Massacres and War of 1862. Adrian J. Ebell.
" XXVIII, p. 76. Overland from St. Paul to Lake Superior. Anon.
" do. p. 190. The Wheat Fields of Minnesota. By G. W. Schatzel.
" XXXVI, p. 409. The Minnesota Pineries. By J. M. Tuttle.

COLLECTIONS OF THE HISTORICAL SOCIETY.

VOLUME I.

1. ANNALS OF THE MINNESOTA HISTORICAL SOCIETY. Saint Paul: Printed by James M. Goodhue. 1850. 8°: pp. 32.
Papers. Preface; Act of Incorporation ; Constitution and By-Laws, adopted Jan. 14, 1850; List of Members; Annual Address by Rev. E. D. Neill, Jan. 1, 1850, Subject—"An Introductory Lecture upon the Subject of the French Voyageurs to this Territory during the Seventeenth Century." Description of Minnesota, by H. H. Sibley; Table of Distances in the Territory.

2. ANNALS OF THE MINNESOTA HISTORICAL SOCIETY, for the year A. D. 1850–1 ; comprising an address by the President,

the Annual Report by the Secretary, two papers by Rev. S. R.
Riggs, &c., &c. St. Paul: D. A. Robertson, Printer. 1851.
8°: pp. 184.

Papers. Proceedings of the Annual Meeting, Jan. 13, 1851; Address of Gov.
A. Ramsey, President of the Society; First Annual Report of C. K. Smith,
Secretary of the Society, with appendices; Speech of Henry H. Sibley, of
Minnesota, before the Com. on Elections of the House of Representatives,
Dec. 22, 1848; List of the Executive and Judicial Officers of the Territory, and
Members of the First Legisature; Titles of Acts passed at the First Session of
the Legislature; List of Officers appointed by the Governor of said Territory;
Do. of the different counties; Time of holding the Courts of Minnesota Ter. ;
Indian Tribes of Minnesota; Description of Saint Paul, and other points in
the Territory; First Navigation of the Minnesota by Steamboats, [June, 1850;]
Fort Snelling; List of Post Offices and Post Masters in Minnesota; Landing
Points for Steamboats from Galena to St. Paul; The Census; Schools and Education in Minnesota; The Fruits and Roots of the Minnesota Valley; Laying
of the Corner Stone of the Episcopal Church; University of Minnesota at the
Falls of St. Anthony; Religious Movements in Minnesota; Table of Steamboat Arrivals, etc., at Fort Snelling for the past six years; The Dakota Nation—Address of Rev. S. R. Riggs; Prospectus for Publishing a Dakota Lexi-
con; A Memoir on the History and Physical Geography of Minnesota, by H.
R. Schoolcraft; the Meteorology of Minnesota, by J. W. Bond; Letter of Prof.
Mather, of Ohio; Index.

3. ANNALS OF THE MINNESOTA HISTORICAL SOCIETY, 1852;
containing the Annual Address by J. H. Simpson, First Lieut.,
Corps, U. S. Topographical Engineers, and other papers. Published by order of the Executive Council. St. Paul: Owens
& Moore, Printers, Minnesotian Office. 8°: pp. 64.

Papers. Secretary's Annual Report; Annual Address by Lieut. Simpson—
"Narrative of a Tour through the Navajo Country ;" Letter of Mesnard, writ-
ten oh the eve of his Embarkation for Lake Superior; Ancient Monuments;
Iowa Indians and Mounds; Letter from Mr. J. F. Aiton on the Stone Heaps
at Red Wing; The Early Nomenclature of Minnesota; Minnesota, its Name
and Origin; Saint Louis River, by Rev. T. M. Fullerton; Sketch of the Early
Indian Trade and Traders of Minnesota, by E. D. Neill; Exploring Tour, by
Rev. W. T. Boutwell; Battle of Lake Pokegama, by "an eye witness;"
Wa-kan-Tibi; Grant of Land at the Cave in Dayton's Bluff.

4. ANNALS OF THE MINNESOTA HISTORICAL SOCIETY, for eigh-
teen hundred and fifty-three: Number IV. Printed by order
of the Executive Council. Saint Paul: Owens & Moore,
Printers. 1853. 8°: pp. 72.

Papers. Officers of the Society for 1853; Annual Report of Secretary; Sketch
of the Life of Nicollet, by Hon. Henry H. Sibley; Sketch of Joseph Renville;
Department of Hudson Bay, by Rev. G. A. Belcourt; Mounds of the Minne-
sota Valley, by Rev. S. R. Riggs; Obituary Notice of James M. Goodhue, late
Editor of the Pioneer; Notes Supplementary to the Early Indian Trade, &c.,
(Annals of 1852 ;) Description of Mille Lacs, by J. G. Norwood, M. D.; Dakota
Land and Dakota Life, by Edward D. Neill; The Meteorology of Minnesota,
by John W. Bond.

5. MATERIALS FOR THE FUTURE HISTORY OF MINNESOTA; being a Report of the Minnesota Historical Society to the Legislative Assembly, in accordance with a Joint Resolution. Fifteen hundred copies ordered to be printed for the use of the Legislature. St. Paul: Joseph R. Brown, Territorial Printer. Pioneer and Democrat Office. 1856. 8°: pp. 142. [7 illustrations.]

Contents. Introductory Chapter, on Nomenclature; Who were the first Men? by Rev. T. S. Williamson; An Historical Review [Reprint of the Address of Gov. Ramsey in 1851;] Early Notices of the Dakotas, by Edward D. Neill; Louis Hennepin, the Franciscan; Sieur Du Luth; Le Sueur, the Explorer of the Minnesota River; Abstract of the Memorial of D'Iberville, on the Country of the Mississippi; Minnesota as a British Dominion—Explorations of Jonathan Carver; British Trade in Minnesota; Pike's Explorations in 1805; American Trade; Noted Early Indian Traders; Fort Snelling; Border Life in Minnesota, by Wm. J. Snelling; Index.

6. ADDRESS delivered before the Minnesota Historical Society, at its Sixth Anniversary, Feb. 1st, 1856, by the Hon. H. H. Sibley. 8°: pp. 17.

[Total number of pages in Vol. I, 511.]

VOLUME II.

1. VOYAGE IN A SIX-OARED SKIFF to the Falls of Saint Anthony in 1817. By Major Stephen H. Long, Topographical Engineer, United States Army. With introductory note by Edward D. Neill, Secretary Minnesota Historical Society. Philadelphia: Henry B. Ashmead, Book and Job Printer. 1860. 8°: pp. 88.

Contents. Officers of the Society; Introductory Note; Journal; Appendix; Map; Letter from A. J. Hill; Table of Distances, &c.

2. COLLECTIONS OF THE MINNESOTA HISTORICAL SOCIETY, for the year 1864. Saint Paul: David Ramaley, Printer. 1865. 8°: pp. 84.

Contents. Officers of the Society; Introductory; Early French Forts and Foot Prints of the Valley of the Upper Mississippi, by E. D. Neill; Occurrences in and around Fort Snelling, from 1819 to 1840, by E. D. Neill; History of the Dakotas—James W. Lynd's Manuscripts, by Rev. S. R. Riggs; the Religion of the Dakotas—(Chapter VI, of Mr. Lynd's Manuscript).

3. COLLECTIONS OF THE MINNESOTA HISTORICAL SOCIETY, for the year 1867. Saint Paul: Pioneer Printing Company. 1867. 8°: pp. 62.

Contents. Officers of the Society; List of Papers; Report of the Committee of Publication; Annual Report of the Secretary, Chas. E. Mayo; Mineral Regions of Lake Superior, as known from their first discovery to 1865, by H. M. Rice; Constantine Beltrami, by A. J. Hill; Historical Notes of the U. S. Land

Office, by H. M. Rice, St. Paul; The Geography of Perrot, so far as it relates to Minnesota and the regions immediately adjacent, by A. J. Hill; Dakota Superstitions, by Rev. G. H. Pond.

4. THE CARVER CENTENARY: An Account of the Celebration, by the Minnesota Historical Society, of the One Hundredth Anniversary of the Council and Treaty of Capt. Jonathan Carver with the Naudowessies, on May 1, 1767, at the "Great Cave" (now within the limits of the City of Saint Paul, Minnesota,) held May 1, 1867. Saint Paul: Pioneer Printing Company. 1867. 8°: pp. 23. With portrait of Carver.

Contents. Preface; The Visit to the Cave; Description of the Cave; The Proceedings at the Cave; The Reunion in the Evening; Paper, by Rev. Jno. Mattocks, on the "Life and Explorations of Jonathan Carver."

5. CHARTER, CONSTITUTION[1] AND BY-LAWS of the Minnesota Historical Society. "Lux e Tenebris." Saint Paul: Ramaley & Hall, Printers. 1868. 8°: pp. 11.

[Total number of pages in Vol. II, 268.]

CHARTER, CONSTITUTION, BY-LAWS AND CATALOGUE OF MEMBERS of the Minnesota Historical Society. MDCCCLVII. Saint Paul: Goodrich, Somers & Co., Printers. 1857. 12°: pp. 43.

INDEX OF AUTHORS.

A.

B.

---

1. Adopted January 20, 1868.

BISHOP, MRS. HARRIET E.—Floral Home.
       The Dakota War Whoop.
       Minnesota, Then and Now.
BISHOP, J. W.—History of Fillmore County.
BLANCHARD, RUFUS—Hand Book of Minnesota.
BOND, J. WESLEY—Minnesota and its Resources.
BREMER, FREDERIKA—The Homes of the New World.
BROOKS, REV. JABEZ—Methodism, a Centenary Sermon.
BRYANT, CHAS. S., (and A. B. MURCH)—History of the Sioux Massacre.
BURRITT, E. H.—Journal of Capt. Fiske's Expedition.

C.

CARVER, JONATHAN—Travels through the Interior Parts of North
  America, &c.
CATLIN, GEORGE—Indians of North America.
CASTLE, HENRY A.—The Problem of American Destiny.
CHAMBERLAIN, H. E.—St. Anthony and Minneapolis Directory.
CHARLEVOIX, F. X.—History of New France.
CHASE, REV. GEO. L.—Christ, not Self. A Sermon.
CHATFIELD, A. G.—Opinion in the Hastings Land Site Case.
CHILD, JAMES E.—Waseca County, &c.
CHITTENDEN, N. H.—Stranger's Guide to Minneapolis.
COFFIN, C. C.—The Great Commercial Prize.
      The Seat of Empire.
COLBURN, MARY J.—Minnesota as a Home for Emigrants.
COLESON, ANN—Narrative of Indian Captivity.
COLONEY, M.—Manomin; a Rhythmical Romance.
COMBS, WM. S.—Revised Journal of Masonic Grand Lodge.
CRAWFORD, I. D.—(See Ketchum, &c.)

D.

DISTURNELL, J.—Tourists' Guide to the Upper Mississippi.
DODGE, O. E.—St. Paul Chamber of Commerce Report, 1870.
DONNELLY, IGNATIUS—Minnesota; an Address, &c.
      The Sonnets of Shakspeare; an Essay.
DU PRATZ, LE PAGE—History of Louisiana.

E.

EASTLICK, MRS. LAVINA—Narrative of Indian Captivity.
EASTMAN, MRS. MARY H.—Dahcotah; or Life and Legends, &c.
      The Romance of Indian Life.
EBELL, ADRIAN J.—The Indian Massacres of 1862. (Harpers' Mag.)
EDWARDS, RICHARD—Gazetteer of the Mississippi River.

F.

FEATHERSTONHAUGH, G. W.—Canoe Voyage up the Minnay Sotor.
FISKE, CAPT. J. L.—Report on his 1st and 2d trips to Idaho.
FOLWELL, WILLIAM W.—Inaugural Address at State University.
FORD, L. M.—Minnesota Farmer and Gardener.
FRENCH, B. F.—Histor. Coll. of La. and Fla.
FRINK, F. W.—A Record of Rice County, &c.

G.

GALE, GEORGE—Upper Mississippi.
GORDON, H. L.—Fourth of July Oration.
GRACE, RT. REV. T. L.—The Papal Encyclical.
GRAY, REV. EDWARD P.—Harmony of the Gospel History.
GRIFFITH, T. M.—(See Anderson, C. L.)
GRISWOLD, WM. B.—Mankato; and Blue Earth County.

H.

HAINES, E. M.—Compilation of Minnesota Laws.
HALL, JAMES—Notes upon the Geology, &c., of Minnesota.
HANKINS, H.—Dakota Land; or Beauty of St. Paul.
HART, REV. BURDETT—Congregationalism. A Sermon.
                The New North-West.
HAWLEY, REV. S.—The Fall of Sumpter.
HEARD, I. V. D.—History of the Sioux War.
                Index to Common Council Proceedings, &c.
HEATON, HON. D.—Manufactures and Trade of the Upper Mississippi.
HENNEPIN, L.—New Discovery of a Great Country, &c.
HEWITT, G.—Minnesota; Its Advantages to Settlers.
HINMAN, REV. S. D.—Calvary Catechism in Dakota.
                Prayer Book translated into Dakota.
                Hymns translated into Dakota.
HUDSON, A. G.—Review of a Sermon on Immortality.

J.

JAMES, DR. EDWIN—Tanner's Narrative of Captivity.
JOHNSON, EDWIN F.—Report on Nor. Pacific R. R.

K.

KEATING, WM. H.—Expedition to Sources of the St. Peters River.
KEILLER, ANDREW—Directory of St. Paul, 1857.
KENNEDY, E. C.—Osseo, the Spectre Chieftain.
KETCHUM, F. A., (and CRAWFORD)—St. Paul Directory, 1869.
KLOOS, J. H.—Dutch Immigration Pamphlet.
                Rapport yan Ingenieur, &c.

L.·

LA HONTAN, BARON—New Voyages to North America.
LANDER, FRED. W.—Report of a R. R. Reconnoisance, &c.
LANMAN, CHAS.—A Summer in the Wilderness.
LATROBE, C. J.—The Rambler in North America.
LEA, ALBERT M.—Notes on Wisconsin Territory.
LE DUC, W. G.—Minnesota Year Books, 1851-2-3.
LISTEO, SOREN—Scandinavian Immigration Pamphlet.
LOGAN, MRS. F. A.—Equal Rights, &c.
LOMBARD, C. W.—History of 3d Minnesota Regiment.
LONG, MAJ. S. H.—Voyage in a six-oared Skiff, &c.
LUBY, M. D. C.—The Columbiad.
LUDDEN, JNO. D.—St. Paul Chamber of Commerce Reports, 1868-69.

M.

MARBLE, MANTON—To Red River and Beyond, (Harpers' Mag.)
MARSHALL, WM. R. (and others)—Statement on Resources of N.P.R.R.
MARSHALL, REV. THOMAS—Dedication Sermon—Mankato.
MATTSON, HON. H.—Scandinavian Immigration Pamphlets.
McCONKEY, MRS. H. E. B.—(See Bishop, Mrs. H. E.)
McCLUNG, J. W.—Saint Paul Directory, 1866.
            Minnesota as it is in 1869.
MERWIN, HEMAN—Minnesota Business Directory.
MITCHELL, W. H.—History of Olmsted County.
            History of Steel County.
            History of Hennepin County.
            History of Goodhue County.
            History of Dakota County.
MUNSON, A D.—Rise and Progress of Minnesota Territory.
MURCH, A. B.—(See Bryant, C. S.)

N.

NEILL, REV. E. D.—Dahkotah Land and Dahkotah Life.
            History of Minnesota.
            Michal; or Fashionable Dancing.
            Hand Book of the Presbyterian Church.
            Effort and Failure to Civilize the Aborigines.
NICHOLS, REV. H. M.—True Thanksgiving; and True Manhood.
NICOLAY, J. G.—Hole-in-the-Day—(Harpers' Mag.)
NICOLLET, J. N.—Hydrographical Basin of Upper Mississippi.
NOBLE, REV. F. A.—Blood, the Price of Redemption.
            The Assured and Glorious Future of the Nation.
NOBLES, COL. WM. H.—Speech on Emigrant Route, &c.

O.

O'BRIEN, DILLON—The Dalys of Dalystown.
OFFICER, HARVEY—Vols. I-IX, Supreme Court Reports.
OLIPHANT, LAURENCE—Minnesota and the Far West.
OWEN, DAVID DALE—Geological Survey of Minnesota.

P.

PARKER, NATHAN H.—The Minnesota Hand Book, 1856-7.
PARKMAN, FRANCIS—The Discovery of the Great West.
PAYNE, W. W.—The Minnesota Teacher.
PELZ, EDWARD—German Immigration Documents.
PERROT, NICOLAS—Memoir on the Manners, &c., of the Indians.
PHELPS, WM. F.—Educational Address.
PIERSON, A. T. C.—Masonic Installation Addresses.
        Lodge of Sorrow Ceremony.
PIKE, Z. M.—Exploration of the Upper Mississippi.
POND, REV. G. H.—Dakota School Books.
POND, REV. S. W.—Translations of Works into Dakota.
POPE, CAPT. JOHN—Exploration of Minnesota Territory.
POPE, REV. JNO. D.—Children and the Childhood of Jesus.
        Anniversary Sermon, &c.
PUSEY, PENNOCK—Statistics of Minnesota, 1870.

R.

RAMSEY, HON. ALEX.—Address at 2d Territorial Fair.
RAVOUX, REV. A.—Path to Heaven, (Dakota).
RAWLINGS, T.—Emigration, with special reference to Minnesota.
RENO, CAPT. J. L.—Survey of a Road from Mendota to the Big Sioux.
RENVILLE, JOHN B.—Translations into Dakota.
RENVILLE, JOSEPH—Translations into Dakota.
RICE, G. J., (and BELL)—St. Paul Directory, 1869.
RIGGS, MRS. M. A. C.—English and Dakota Dictionary.
RIGGS, REV. STEPHEN R.—Grammar and Dictionary of the Dakota
        Language.
        Translations and Works in Dakota.
        Tah-Koo-Wah Kan, or Gospel among the
        Dakotas.
RITZ, PHILIP—Letter on the new route, (to the Pacific).
ROBERTSON, D. A.—The Minnesota Monthly.
ROSA, GABRIELE—Life of Constantine Beltrami.

S.

SAMPLE, REV. R. T.—Historical Sketch of Westminster Presb. Ch.
SCHATZEL, G. W.—The Wheat Fields of Minnesota—(Harper's Mag.)
10

SCHOOLCRAFT, H. R.—Indian Tribes of the United States.
> Narrative of Travels from Detroit, N. W., &c.
> Narrative of an Expedition to Itasca Lake in 1820.
> Summary of an Expedition to Itasca Lake in 1832.
> Thirty years' residence with the Indian Tribes.

SEYMOUR, E. S.—Sketches of Minnesota; the N. E. of the West.

SHAW, E. P.—Minneapolis Directory.

SHEA, JOHN G.—Discovery and Exploration of the Mississippi.
> Early Voyages up and down the Mississippi.

SHIELDS, HON. JAMES—Speech on Pacific Railroad Bill.

SKINNER, REV. D.—The Final Salvation of all Mankind.

SMITH, HON. A. C.—Masonic Installation Address.

SMITH, FRANCIS H.—Official Report of Constitutional Convention, (Democratic Wing.)

SMITH, W. R.—Minnesota as a Home for Immigrants.

SORIN, REV. M.—Political Character of Romanism.

SPENCER, WM. A.—Vols. X to XIII, Supreme Court Reports.

STARKEY, JAMES—Suggestions as to Sewerage &c., in St. Paul.

STEVENS, ISAAC I.—Northern Pacific R. R. Survey, Vol. XII.
> Letter on Northern Pacific Route.

STEVENS, REV. J. D.—Dakota Spelling Book.

STEVENS, JNO. H.—Early History of Hennepin County.

STONE, REV. GEO. M.—Life of Dr. John D. Ford.

STORRY, W. D.—A view of Saint Anthony Falls.

SWEETZER, CHAS. H.—Tourist's and Invalid's Guide to the N. W.

T.

TAYLOR, JAS. W.—The Railroad System of Minnesota.
> North-West British America.
> The Sioux War; What shall we do with it?
> The Sioux War; Campaign of 1863.

TUTTLE, REV. J. B.—Universalism Unmasked.

TUTTLE, J. M.—The Minnesota Pineries.

V.

VAN INGEN, REV. J. V.—Memorial, &c., on Church Foundation.

W.

WAKEFIELD, MRS. SARAH F.—Six weeks in the Sioux Teepes.

WARREN, GEN. G. K.—Reports on Survey of Upper Mississippi.
> Physical Features of the Upper Miss. Valley.

WEEKS, MRS. HELEN C.—White and Red.

WHEELOCK, JOS. A.—Minnesota; Its Place among the States.
> Minnesota; Its Progress and Capabilities.

WHIPPLE, RT. REV. H. B.—Address to the 10th Convention, &c.

WHITTLESEY, CHAS.—Geology and Minerals.
WILKINSON, M. S.—Revised Statutes of 1851.
WILLARD, J. A.—Blue Earth Co.; its Advantages, &c.
WILLIAMS, REV. EDWIN SIDNEY—Christian Amusements. A Sermon.
WILLIAMS, J. F.—Carver Centenary.
              Early History of St. Paul.
              Reports of Historical Society, 1868-9-70.
              The Minnesota Guide.
              Atlantic Cable Celebration, St. Paul.
WILLIAMSON, REV. T. S.—Translations into Dakota.
              Discourse before Synod of Minnesota.
WILLIAMSON, JOHN P.—Dakota School Books, etc.
WINDOM, WM.—Speech on Nor. Pac. R. R. Bill.
WINSTON, T. B.—Minnesota—a bundle of facts, &c.
WOLFF, ALBERT—Gedichte Vermischten Inhalts.
WOLFE, J. M.—Winona Directory.
WOODS, MAJ. S.—Pembina Settlement, &c.

*** The foregoing article was completed February, 1870, and includes only books issued up to that time.